THE LAST CRUISE OF THE
"MAJESTIC"

Reproduced by permission of] [*The Daily Mail.*

LANDING TROOPS AND HORSES AT THE DARDANELLES.

Frontispiece]

THE LAST CRUISE OF THE "MAJESTIC"

BY
GEORGE GOODCHILD

From the log-book of
Ex-Petty Officer J. G. COWIE, H.M.S. "Majestic"

The Naval & Military Press Ltd

Published by

The Naval & Military Press Ltd
Unit 5 Riverside, Brambleside
Bellbrook Industrial Estate
Uckfield, East Sussex
TN22 1QQ England

Tel: +44 (0)1825 749494

www.naval-military-press.com
www.nmarchive.com

*In reprinting in facsimile from the original, any imperfections are inevitably reproduced
and the quality may fall short of modern type and cartographic standards.*

CONTENTS

CHAPTER I

MOBILISATION 11   PAGE

CHAPTER II

UP CHANNEL WITH A PRIZE . . . 21

CHAPTER III

H.M.S. "MAJESTIC" 30

CHAPTER IV

ON A NEW MISSION 44

CHAPTER V

BOMBARDING THE BELGIAN COAST . . 52

CONTENTS

CHAPTER VI

	PAGE
EASTWARD BOUND	60

CHAPTER VII

THE DARDANELLES	69

CHAPTER VIII

THE GENERAL BOMBARDMENT	85

CHAPTER IX

AFTER THE BOMBARDMENT	102

CHAPTER X

THE GREAT LANDING	121

CHAPTER XI

BACK TO THE DARDANELLES . . . 139

CHAPTER XII

LOSS OF H.M.S. "GOLIATH" . . . 150

CHAPTER XIII

THE LOSS OF THE "TRIUMPH" . . . 161

CHAPTER XIV

THE LAST OF THE "MAJESTIC" . . . 169

CHAPTER XV

HOME AGAIN 180

THE LAST CRUISE OF THE "MAJESTIC"

CHAPTER I

MOBILISATION

FOR me the war was ushered in by the buzzing of a telephone. Thousands of times had I answered that telephone, and never a message to relieve the even tenor of my life. Yet never had I quite convinced myself that my (day) had gone beyond recall and that the reshaping of nations was relegated to a future generation. I think there was always a kind of premonition that life held something " fast and furious " in store for me, and it was the telephone-bell that first confirmed that suspicion and set my feet on the war-path.

Excitedly I wrote the message down :

" From C.O. to all stations. Crew to be ready to catch first train in the morning for R.N.B. Devonport. All gear to be taken."

That was all. Not a very communicative message, but sufficient to set a man's heart beating faster. The man at the other end jerked out the syllables so incoherently that I hardly recognised his voice, though I had listened to it for months. I could imagine his face red with uncontrollable eagerness and could hear the quick intake of the breath between the words.

" Got that ? " he cried.

" Yes ! Right-o ! See you at the station. Off to pack now."

" Are you detailed for a ship ? "

" No."

" Neither am I."

" What do you make the time ? "

" What ? Twelve o'clock ! That means no relief to-night, since we must leave at five o'clock in the morning. Ta-ta ! "

And so he left me, a little uncertain whether I was pleased or not. At first thought it is natural for a man to be overjoyed when a quarter of a century has been spent on fighting ships, traversing the waterways of the world. It was my " day " that was coming—the " day " that every Navy man knew must come sooner or later. It was the great Naval " Derby " for which the

Service had been in training since the time when the Teuton first dreamt of a world hegemony, and had visions of a greater Germany.

Yet God forbid that I should eagerly welcome the Armageddon; there is the other side to be considered—misery and sorrow unending—great ships with a thousand souls dropped like a stone to oblivion. I cannot think that callousness is a necessary quality of the fighting man. We shall do better to remember the human side. We shall fight better if we feel that only by doing so shall such a conflagration be made impossible in the future.

As in a dream I packed my bag and then, meditating upon the inscrutable future, almost forgot to call the "bhoys" up. It afforded me some little amusement to see the blank look of surprise in their faces when I had knocked them out of their peaceful slumbers. The first question in every case was " what the hell I meant by waking them up like that, when I knew it wasn't their watch"! But nothing could express their amazement when they learned that they must catch the 6 a.m. train from Churston.

It was all hurry-scurry then—endless oddments that really didn't matter, and yet were so dear to a man's heart, being crammed into bags. Then, of course, there was a bombardment of questions from the womenfolk, some to be answered, some to be evaded. " Would England go to war ? Would England go to war ? " That seemed to be the vital question with them, and that was the most difficult to answer—although it was the one we could probably answer most easily. However, it didn't seem a wise thing to do, so we assured them that we were merely being called up as a precautionary measure, and that we hoped to be home for the week-end—Heaven forgive us !

The boys seemed tremendously excited, and I knew by the grin on their ugly old faces that they rather fancied a bout with the " Hun." A car had been ordered to take us to the station, and in the middle of a further embarrassing bombardment of questions it arrived and saved the situation. A hand-shake, a kiss, that recurring nasty little lump in the throat which *will* persist in turning up, and off we went down the hill, vibrating and jolting alarmingly. Thus we four—Jeff, Harry, Billy, and myself—

started on the great adventure. A trip through a beautiful piece of dear old England on a summer morn, with the fluffy-tailed rabbits scampering almost under the wheels of the car, and the trees setting up a peaceful musical murmur in the soft breeze seemed in extraordinary contrast with the thoughts that teemed in our brains. I suppose we all felt keener by the sight of those rural delights. There seemed something tangible to fight for, and I was glad that my particular "bit" lay on the sea that girdled our little island. At the station we met more Coastguards that had been called up to mobilise, so we all proceeded together to the R.N.B., Devonport. Even at the station I was surprised to find that the majority of opinion was that we should not go to war. It seemed to me amazing that people could hold such opinions—personally I never doubted that the day was coming when the Teuton would put out the "mailed" fist, and I knew that the "enemy" was England, and that the Navy had been in training for this time.

We arrived at Devonport at 10 a.m., were told off into Messes, and then drew bedding—blankets and hammock. A few other C.G. ratings were there already from nearer stations. These had previously been "told off" for ships before coming up, and were standing by to proceed at a moment's notice. I felt very disappointed not to have been "told off" for a ship, and didn't relish the idea of lamely standing by.

In an hour or two men were streaming into the Barracks: Coast Guards, Royal Fleet Reserves, and Royal Naval Reserves, all looking very grim and determined. In the afternoon there was a general assembly to muster men "told off" for ships, and to despatch them to their various destinations. I watched them go, and felt sick at standing about like a tame cat, so I turned into my hammock early.

The next day (July 30th) was a "wash out" so far as I was concerned. We mustered early on the Parade-ground, and I with others was told off to go coaling ships in "Docky." Not much of a game, coaling ships, but fine for the appetite, and better still as a sleeping-draught.

Paraded no less than three times next day, but no luck for yours truly. I began to wonder whether I was ear-marked for a post in the Admiralty, until I realised what a shocking loss that would be to the Navy.

MOBILISATION

Drafts of men were going off all day, and Reserves of all classes were coming in by the hundred. There is always something fascinating in watching a mobilisation of men, especially when one is of the same service. I believe one could detail their various ratings by the set of their faces. I found myself sorting them out into categories —stokers, gunners, signallers, and so forth, and then from the sea of faces would come one I knew well, and there was the usual " Well, I'm——" and a quick summary of the past. I met several old " ships " that day, and all seemed glad to be going afloat. Many of the men had been travelling all night from the remotest spots of England, but there was not one that had not a pleased expression and a cheery smile. A good many had no hammocks to sleep in, but they never complained, for all knew what a big task it was to " kit up " thousands of men like this at a moment's notice. They all waited patiently for their turn to come, and in the meantime many of them spread out newspapers and went to sleep on them. The Canteen, which had been converted into a kind of Receiving-room, was full of them.

Writers and ships were having a busy

time, for the stream of men never ceased. Hour after hour they streamed in from every part of the kingdom.

The next day (August 1st) was very similar to the day before in all respects. A lot of crews were sent away to ships. Twice I volunteered, but luck was not my way. The R.N.B. was crowded out with men "kitted up." The Paymaster and his staff were heavy-eyed and weary, not having left their office the whole night. In the morning I learned that our ultimatum to Germany would expire at midnight. There were crowds everywhere waiting to hear the result. After midnight they still thronged the streets, and then, as the hours went by and no news came, the drone of conversation grew less and the streets grew silent as the throng went home to their beds—and I to mine.

August 2nd.—Still no further news of the ultimatum. Could it mean that Germany was going to climb down ? Some men seemed to think so, but even my limited intelligence knew better than that. Still men came in—men, men, men from every conceivable corner of the land. Men with hard, bronzed faces, men with the typical Jack Tar countenance, men who had followed

MOBILISATION

the sea from childhood, men who had waited, as I had waited, for the great day. And all cheerful and sober, thank God! What men these were!—from the quiet little villages in the shires, from the great grey cities, from factory and warehouses, plough and harrow, all back to the vast, free, wind-swept element that first breathed liberty into their souls. Here they were, 25,000 of Britain's best, filling every place from cellar to attic, joyful in the one transcending emotion that swayed them—the spindrift in their nostrils and the fear of God in their souls.

In the evening luck came my way for the space of twenty minutes. I was told off for ss. "Coronia," only to discover later that the number of men had been miscalculated, and that I must continue to stand by.

And so I stood by for about a fortnight, hoping every day that my little goddess of luck would come in my direction; but she never came. The only things that came continuously were men, men, men. Every day I mustered with them, and every day I seemed to miss a ship by an inch. Heaven knows who manages these things, but there you are!

The war had started, and the German hosts were flinging themselves against heroic little Belgium, as it was almost inevitable they would do. The days passed quick enough with the constant arrival of men and the thrilling news that came from the Belgian frontier, but how I longed for a ship. And then all unexpectedly it came.

CHAPTER II

UP CHANNEL WITH A PRIZE

It is rather humiliating, when one has fondly visualised a fine modern Dreadnought, to be shoved on board a German steamship, but that was my particular luck.

She was a prize ship, the " Prinz Adalbert," caught in the Atlantic and brought to Falmouth, where we were told to join her for the purpose of taking her up the Thames. We mustered at 1 a.m. with hammocks and bags all ready for departure, and then failed to get any official instructions, so dismissed and hung about all day. At 9 p.m. we paraded again, and were told to fall in at 6.30 the next morning. Considerably " fed up " with the delay, I turned into my hammock and slept the sleep of the just.

At 6.30 punctually next morning the prize crew paraded—75 in all, including officers. To my intense delight, I was appointed signalling officer, which was very much to my liking. We dismissed to get breakfast and to get the luggage down to the station, and then at 10 a.m. we departed for Falmouth. On the train we met another prize crew also bound for Falmouth to man the "Kron Princessen Cicellie," that had suffered the same fate as the "Prinz Adalbert." We broke the journey at Truro, the old city of Cornwall, and had lunch, which consisted of a good "Teddy Hoggie" pasty, ham sandwiches, and a pint of the best "home brewed."

At Falmouth a tug took us off to the "Prinz Adalbert," and I spent an interesting five minutes in running my eyes over her lines. She was certainly a fine ship, and the Germans must have been mighty sick at losing her. We took the ship over from some Territorials and ship-keepers, got our kits aboard, and bedded-down for the night.

Looking over the prize the following morning, I found her to be even a better ship than I had at first realised. She was fitted up in truly gorgeous style, with every convenience possible to imagine. She was in all respects a floating hotel. Four of us—myself and three leading seamen of the

R.N.R.—took the Quartermaster's mess abaft the fore bridge. This we found to be admirable in every way, and quite near to the bridge for signalling purposes. At 8 a.m. I went aft and hoisted the White Ensign over the German colours to denote that the ship was a prize.

I was surprised to find that the ship had been left in very good condition, all things considered, for the German crew had been left on board for a week and could have caused any amount of damage had they chosen to. Why they did not, Heaven only knows.

The engineers were hard at work down below getting her ready for sea. Now and again the pleasant clank of hammers came up—a sound like music to a man who has been bred in that atmosphere. In the harbour were several smaller German prizes, and just ahead of us the American battleship "Carolina."

The next morning (August 22nd) we were still at anchor, waiting for the engineers to get the engines going. The difficulty appeared to be our astounding ignorance of languages. None of the engineers understood German, and of course all the markings and instructions were in German. Late at night they overcame the difficulties, and the engine commenced throbbing at last.

We reported "ready for sea" to the authorities and were ordered to proceed in the morning in company with the "Kron Princessen Cicellie."

In the morning we were all ready; we tested the compass and other nautical instruments, and then at 11 a.m. slipped the buoy. Our speed was very slow—about 6 knots—as the engineers were still unacquainted with all the details of the machinery. The weather was very thick, and we were constantly challenged by destroyers, some of which came right up to us. No doubt we looked a pretty suspicious kettle of fish.

We soon parted company with the "Kron Princessen," who was sick of our crawling pace, and wanted to forge ahead. All the way up the Channel T.B.D.'s were challenging us, and, one of them not being satisfied, despite the fact that her challenge was answered correctly, fired a shot across our bows. The captain had a few words to say about that, and then stuck me on the bridge and told me to remain there till we got into the Thames.

UP CHANNEL WITH A PRIZE

Off Portsmouth we were called into the Bay to be examined, and, after being detained two hours, we wended our way up Channel again. About every hour we were challenged, so I had a fairly lively time of it all through the night. Luckily the weather kept fine, and not too cold at night.

At 4 a.m. we arrived off Dover and shipped a pilot who was going to take us up the Downs as far as the Nore Lightship, where we were to wait until we received further orders from the Admiralty.

I was overjoyed to hear from the pilot that the " Kron Princessen " had not passed up yet. It certainly looked as though the " lame duck " had beaten her.

All up the Downs T.B.D.'s were lying thick as herrings, and we were challenged, stopped, and examined times without number: We eventually reported ourselves to the Nore Lightship, where we received orders to proceed to the West India Docks.

Just as we were leaving the " Kron Princessen " hove into sight, and I could imagine the chagrin of her captain to find us looming on his horizon. Still, we had our instructions, so we steamed merrily up the river.

Southend Pier and beach were crowded

with people who had by some means discovered that the ship was a German prize, and they cheered themselves hoarse in their enthusiasm. And well they might, for it was the first German prize that had ever been taken up good old Father Thames.

This was my first trip up the Thames, so I stayed on the bridge the whole time in order that I might see the sights all the way up. I can't say that I was very much impressed. It has no comparison with many of our ports that lie on the other side of the globe. It is all so drab and dingy, with no outstanding features that one might remember. Nothing that sticks in the mind's eye to create one of those lasting images that never depart.

At 5 p.m. we arrived at the West India Docks, and were soon docked and tied up for the night in one of those inner basins of the Dock. In the morning a crowd of stevedores came aboard to discharge the cargo.

For the next fortnight I remained with the ship while the cargo was being put ashore. During this period I had many opportunities of seeing the great hub of the universe about which I had heard so much.

It was a bitter disappointment for me—

this great London. I could see little in it to shout about. For the most part it was dirty and muddy. All the houses and buildings seemed smoke-begrimed, and the more I saw of it the less I liked it.

One never seemed to be able to get out of it. It was like a great octopus sprawling its miles of street and warehouse, shop and tram-line, and it had a sombre air which had a tendency to damp my spirits.

It may have seemed thus because I had country air in my blood, and because the England which I knew and loved was not of dingy streets and gloomy houses, but something fresher and sweeter. I think I would rather visualise my England as a green little garden with fields and meadows, and verdant woodlands, and neat little whitewashed farms, with the great green engirdling sea lying just beyond the hill.

That was certainly the England that my father knew, and my father's father—and it was that same little England which sings across half the world and shimmers in the waters of some foreign port when a man is afloat. I think I hate the great cities, with the toiling millions like so many imprisoned souls doing penance for something.

It seemed to me that here men were divested of their manhood, that in the faces of each and all was a spirit of unrest, that their minds were part of the huge, mighty machinery.

Oh no! Your London will never call me as I know it calls some men. Is it because of something lacking with me?—or because those who feel its influence and strange fascination have never seen the other England? It may be that. I somehow think it is.

On September 9th I left the ship and took train from Paddington to Devonport. I was sorry to leave the " Prinz Adalbert " —German though she was. A man soon gets to form an attachment with the ship that he lives and sleeps in, and the " Prinz " was certainly conducive to comfort.

Arrived at the R.N.B., Devonport, I returned all my stores, went through the usual medical examination, and then joined the signalling school for instructional purposes: I remained in the school until September 15th, then my ship came along—my real ship.

Little did I dream then of the paths into which fate would fling me. And I think, had I the opportunity, I would not have looked into the future. It is the one thing that makes life worth living—the strange uncertainty of what waits before one—the knowledge that a span of life has to be passed, and the sublime ignorance as to how and in what conditions it is to be weathered.

CHAPTER III

H.M.S. " MAJESTIC "

It was on September 15th, at 11.30 a.m., that I was told off to join the " Majestic," and it was in the nature of a small shock for me, for the old " Majestic " wasn't exactly a palace, still it was certainly better than the R.N.B., which is not altogether a bed of roses at the best of times, to say the least of it. I got all my gear together and left at noon with three other men. We had been told that the " Majestic " was to sail immediately, but when we arrived at the jetty we learned that she was not sailing that day as she was coaling.

What a reception! It had been raining hard all day, and the flying coal-dust, with the rain, formed a compound like blacking everywhere. My one hope was to find a lot of old " ships," but to my keen disappointment I only found two men that I knew.

H.M.S. "MAJESTIC"

Down below she looked a pitiful wreck. The poor old ship had been stripped of all spars, wood-work, etc., and seemed to exhale an atmosphere of misery; but I guessed I was looking at the worst aspect of her, and that a good wash-down would give her a better appearance.

Anyhow, it seemed that all my fond dreams of a dazzling new Dreadnought were doomed to be vain. There was certainly nothing "tremendous" about the old "Majestic." She was the oldest battleship but one in the Service, being laid down in 1894. Her displacement was 14,900 tons. She mounted 4 12-inch and 12 6-inch guns, and steamed at a modest $17\frac{1}{2}$ knots when in the heyday of her youth. But now!—I hesitated to compute what her forward progression might be. She carried a crew of 757, and her side armour was 9-inch thick. In addition, she carried a few small guns and five torpedo tubes.

I stowed away my bags and hammock and set about making the acquaintance of my messmates, a job which turned out to be a very pleasant and successful one.

Later I was detailed for the middle watch on the bridge, which rather upset my calculations, as I had a lot of washing to collect on shore, and had also intended meeting my wife, who had come down to Devonport. I learned, to my great disappointment, that no one was allowed ashore until the ship had finished coaling, which would be about 7.30 p.m. That made the trip impossible, so I was doomed not to see my wife before I sailed. It seemed very hard to me, but I comforted myself with the reflection that this was war, and that thousands of men were experiencing the same inconveniences and disappointments.

I kept my "watch" and found it a very unexciting business, but I was fortunate enough to have an admirable fellow for watch-mate, which was something to be thankful for. The next morning at 8 a.m. we left the jetty and proceeded to sea. Our job was Channel patrol, and we had instructions to join up with other ships of the line, including some French ships, and patrol from Wolf Light to Start Point.

All the hands now turned to and were soon busily engaged in making the ship clean as a new pin. I had now had opportunity of overhauling the whole crew, but beyond the two "old ships" I have mentioned, who served with me in the "Pique" out in China during the Boxer rising, I never found a soul that I knew.

For the next two days we patrolled up and down with not a scrap of luck to encourage us, but on the third day, just after dinner, the mast-head look-out man reported "sail ahead." For the first time we began to experience a little thrill of excitement. There was a fair wind up Channel, and all sails were drawing, so it wasn't long before she came close up to us. We challenged her and told her to hoist her colours. In a twinkling up went the German ensign. What-o! The old war-horse had actually captured a prize, the first in her life. We signalled her to "heave to," but her captain, who doubtless began to smell a rat, proceeded up Channel under all possible sail. We let her rip a couple of blank "charges," but still she kept on her course. Doubtless her captain preferred to think that we were merely practising gunnery, but any such illusion was quickly shattered by our "loosing" a shell right under his very nose. This was the first "angry" shot that the old "Majestic" had ever fired, and I fancied I could feel her sides quivering from the pleasure and pride of it. The German skipper very soon hove to, and we lowered a cutter with a prize crew aboard, and took possession of her.

She turned out to be a barque called " Ponape," and her skipper had the shock of his life when he learned that his dear ship was a prize. Judging by his countenance, the idea of Germany being at war with England had never crept into his unimaginative brain. He seemed very cut up about it all, and explained that he was eighty-four days out of Iqique, loaded with saltpetre; hence his sublime ignorance.

Very sorrowfully he imparted the knowledge to his crew. And what a crew! Germans, Belgians, Frenchmen, Russians, Swedes, Danes, all went to make up the assortment. The Belgians all got very excited, but the rest seemed to take it very seriously. We pulled down the German flag and planted the good old British flag with the German ensign below it, and proceeded to Falmouth with our trophy in tow. Arrived at Falmouth, we left the " Ponape " in charge of a lot of " Terriers " and got to sea again in search of further spoil.

We patrolled up and down the Channel

until September 25th without anything of moment happening, and only those who have done it can really understand how monotonous it becomes when there is " nothing doing." The only way to kill time is to work, and there is never need to seek far for work aboard ship. Hands were put on to cleaning up decks, while some were busy instructing gun crews. "Chipping paintwork" is another harmless form of amusement. It is, however, a very necessary operation, for when a ship is in action the paint is liable to cause fires.

Having now had good time to thoroughly overhaul the old ship, I was surprised to find what a veritable museum she was. Her crew were mixed, to say the least of it, ranging from young boys to pensioners, with a lot of R.N.R. and R.F.R. men. She was apparently blessed with a splendid captain and a fine navigating officer, but some of the others looked as though they required a little tempering in the furnace. However, time proves all things, and it is a foolish operation attempting to estimate the value of a man before he has a chance of proving himself.

On September 26th we left the line and

proceeded to Devonport, where we devoured what little news there was of the progress of the war.

The next day (Sunday) we proceeded up harbour for coaling and revictualling ship, a job which took the whole day and covered one with filth and grime. So much for the Sabbath in war-time. I was dying for a trip ashore in the evening, and managed to get there, but it was the briefest possible trip, for we had to get aboard early. The old town looked much as usual, the most noticeable feature being the enormous number of "knuts" who promenaded the streets.

On the 29th we put to sea again for an unknown destination. Of course, the usual wild rumours were flying around. First, we were off to Canada to bring back troops, then it was South Africa. One soon gets used to disregarding rumours; not one of them ever seems to come true, and yet there is always the tendency to put forward some possible object and to vaguely hint that it comes from official quarters.

We passed the patrol line with a great feeling of relief. At any rate, we were finished with the "up and down" business!

For the next two days we kept our head

down Channel out into the Atlantic, and rumours multiplied like microbes in cheese. On October 1st we sighted a ship which turned out to be the Holland-American liner " Potsdam." We ordered her to heave to and sent a prize crew aboard her to examine her papers. Apparently her papers were not in every way satisfactory, and I was told to board her and take her back to Falmouth, R.N.R. Lieutenant Walker in charge.

We were soon under way and up Channel again with a prize crew of one chief P.O., 12 men, myself, and the lieutenant. We were treated in royal style by the officers and crew. The captain gave orders that we were to be victualled from the ship's stores, and that a special place should be reserved for us to mess in, with a couple of mess-men to look after us. Naturally the biscuits and " bully " we had brought with us was immediately consigned to the nether regions.

The captain and I were on excellent terms, as I used to be at a Lloyd's Station from which he usually signalled home. Cigars and such minor luxuries were accordingly plentiful.

There turned out to be only two German

reserves among the passengers, and these the captain said were really stowaways that he found after the ship had left port. The passengers consisted chiefly of Dutch and Belgians homeward bound, with the customary spattering of Americans, without which no liner's passenger list is complete. Strangest of all, there were two German ladies aboard, one of whom was no less a person than the wife of the first mate of my first prize—the " Prinz Adalbert."

We made the Channel, after signalling Land's End to let the King's Proctor know of our arrival, and reached Falmouth about midnight. We were challenged by the examination boat, who then went ashore to report us. Then the military patrol came aboard and also left to make its report to Headquarters, and so on and so on. Early in the morning a military picket removed the two German reserves, and arrangements were made for taking over the ship from us. At 11 a.m. a party of "Terriers" arrived under two officers and we were relieved just in time to catch the noon train to Devonport.

Later I heard that the " Potsdam " was taken to London and her cargo confiscated by the prize court, as it was proven to be contraband. So our little "catch" was really a valuable one, and the old "warhorse" was justifying her existence!

We arrived at the R.N.B. at six p.m. looking for all the world like a band of "Cornish Pirates of Old," armed to the teeth with revolvers, cutlasses, and rifles. They didn't quite seem to know what to do with us, so in a moment of commendable sympathy gave us "leave" till the morning.

The next day we were told we should have to remain at the barracks until the "Majestic" came back with the Canadians. (So rumour *was* true after all!)

Then for ten weary days I mustered three times daily on the square—a job which I consider the most detestable in life. But I was free every evening, and that went a long way towards ameliorating my woes.

On October 14th I heard that the "Majestic" had arrived in the Sound, and my joy knew no bounds. Very soon we were in the barrack launch heading down stream. What a sight met our eyes! Troopship after troopship was thronging the harbour, and every one of them crowded with soldiers.

It made a wonderful picture in the clear

morning light, a scene which no artist could ever hope to reproduce. I counted thirty-two of them in all; some were well-known liners carrying a couple of thousand men apiece, others were less dignified craft, but all seemed to have an air of pride which in the circumstances was thoroughly justified, for they presented a very gay sight.

Reds, browns, and greens were strangely mixed with the blue background and the bluer sky; quaint noises, syrens blowing, chains rattling, and above all the great drone of men's voices mingled with an occasional mighty cheer. A magnificent sight, and one that I shall never forget.

So this was the Armada that the old "Majestic" was helping to convoy across the Atlantic! Well might she be proud of herself, for the crossing had been successful in every way. I heard there had been but one casualty with the troops, and that merely an internal complaint which would probably have occurred in any case.

On getting aboard I learned that one of my old ship-mates had been lost on the journey out. There was a tremendous sea running at the time, so that there was not much hope for him; but, despite the terrible conditions, an attempt was made to save him by our commander, Michael Barnes, R.N., who saw the man fall. He never hesitated a moment, but went straight overboard after him.

There are some things in life which make a man feel proud he is a man, and this is one of them. Sentimentalism is tabooed in the Service, and such things are taken for granted; but it would be a peculiar man who did not feel a great throb at his breast at such moments.

The commander could do very little in that sea, but he fought pluckily against it and sought for the man in vain. The lifeboat was manned by volunteers, and they eventually succeeded in picking him up, but my old ship-mate had been gathered to his last resting-place, and I daresay it was the kind of death he would have chosen, short of being actually killed in action, which is not every one's luck.

I received some vivid accounts of the journey out from various members of the crew. Throughout the whole voyage the ship was swept by tremendous seas. Everything was wet through, and every grain of comfort knocked out of her. The canteen had "run out," and every one was on "hard tack." It seemed that I was fortunate in my escape.

At 5 p.m. we proceeded up harbour to coal, and were subjected to volley upon volley of cheering.

By the evening of the following day we had coaled ship and cleaned up, so we watched the troopships discharging their cargo.

The Canadian troops were magnificent men, full of high spirits and fun. They were all bitterly disappointed when they learned that they were not going to France at once, but were to go into training before going overseas. By the look of them they would render a very good account of themselves.

We remained in harbour until the 20th and spent a really interesting time in watching the landing of the mass of material which the ships contained—baggage, guns, horses, and the thousand and one items which are a necessity to the waging of war.

Then we commenced our old monotony— patrol duty; but although we steamed up and down, up and down, for three days, not a single blessed German came to gladden our eyes.

On the 23rd we left the patrol line and proceeded to Devonport, where we coaled and had our 12-inch guns renewed, the latter operation causing some little excitement amongst us, for ships do not have brand-new 12-inch guns for nothing. Things looked more promising.

CHAPTER IV

ON A NEW MISSION

ON the 28th we proceeded to sea in company with H.M.S. "Jupiter," and headed up Channel. There was great speculation among the crew, and the usual rumours sufficient in themselves to fill a volume. What added fuel to the rumours was the fact that we had taken on board a quantity of torpedo-netting for boom defence.

All went well until we passed the Straits of Dover, when we had a fine scare. Late in the afternoon the "Jupiter" reported enemy submarines about, and vouchsafed the information that a torpedo had been fired at her, but had missed her. Then a little later a torpedo came skimming towards our own ship. Fortunately for us, we were on a zig-zag course, and the thing went 100 yards wide of us. For a few minutes there was great excitement, but it soon died down when the dose was not repeated. Anyhow, it was quite near enough for my liking.

Farther down Channel an escort of destroyers picked us up and commenced steaming all round us like mad. There is a deal of comfort to be got out of those wicked little black craft, and although we kept a good look-out the U-boats seemed to be tucked away safely under the surface.

Running up the Downs, we made for Sheerness where we tied up to a buoy for the time being, as we had orders to proceed to Chatham Docks to get fitted with "torpedo boom defence." Then our trouble would commence beyond doubt. There is never any lack of cursing with those damned things about, and skin and hair and fingernails flying as a consequence.

It was quite obvious that we were having those things fitted, not to stop torpedoes, which they are powerless to do, but just because the public needed pacifying.

"It's all right, Harry," says an old shipmate. "We're safe now—got torpedo-nets aboard—don't yer know." And Harry spits savagely over the side and so eloquently expresses the sentiments of us all.

We proceeded to Chatham, that dingy,

ugly town, and went into the basin where the booms were fitted for the nets.

We had been in Chatham about four days when some really remarkable news came— a German fleet was coming down the North Sea making for the Straits of Dover. Now any one but a mere idiot would have sniffed at the mere idea of it, but I suppose we were all a little insane just then ; at any rate, out of dock we went like mad, with every soul aboard crazy with excitement. What if it was merely the old " Majestic " ! No one seemed to care a button. Oh, we were a merry little party just then and went down stream with a fine sense of delight. Alas! we were stopped at Sheerness and told to stand by until further notice. Everybody looked blue at that, as it meant that we should have to get our nets properly finished after all.

Our " spud nets " were fitted at Sheerness, and during the time we lay there we had the pleasure of witnessing innumerable seaplane flights and also a few flights by airships, which were a new thing to us. We also saw the monitors come over from the Belgian coast, and also the old " Rinaldo," that ancient crock which did so much good work across the Channel.

ON A NEW MISSION

Who ever would have believed that such vessels would have been brought into service again ! In this super-Dreadnought age one would have imagined that such antiquated craft would have been scrapped, and yet good work has been done by them, and the example helps to ram home the adage concerning "respect for the aged."

Our net defence finished, we received sailing orders for November 15th, and on that day proceeded to sea again with the "Jupiter," which had also been fitted out with "torpedo boom defence." We cleared the Nore Lightship, and were picked up by a T.B.D. flotilla, which informed us that they had come to escort us as far as the Humber.

We passed several men-of-war and patrol boats on the way out and were soon clear of the Thames. Everything went well until about 8 p.m., when we got orders to proceed to Yarmouth Roads and to get out torpedo-nets, as submarines were in the vicinity. With lights covered off, we went full steam ahead for the Roads, and, arriving there, came to anchor. Then came the order "Out nets," and out nets we did—but how we did it, God only knows. It was inky black and most of the crew had never seen a torpedo-net in their lives; then, with the exception of a very, very little help from a small capstan, the whole thing had to be done by hand—a business which is guaranteed to make even a parson profane.

At daybreak we took in those wretched nets and went off for the Humber at full steam. Nothing of interest happened on the way; we passed several mine-sweepers and patrol boats at their arduous work, and arrived off the Humber at 7 p.m. There was no trouble at getting into the river, so we went up as far as Grimsby and anchored at about 8 p.m.

On the following day we were ordered to take up a proper position and to "out nets." What a day! From a leaden sky the rain came down in a deluge. But work had to be done, rain or no rain, so we stuck at it, looking like a community of drowned rats. But no one seemed to be out of temper, which is surprising, seeing that nothing is so miserable as a thorough soaking. I suppose the equable temper of the men was in some measure due to the thought that, at any rate, they were free from submarine menace. After a long struggle the nets were got out, and a huge cheer went up when the men

ON A NEW MISSION

knew they could go below and get some dry clothing.

There was another man-of-war in the river—H.M.S. "Victorious," which was the port guardship, but by all appearances the "Majestic" was going to stay there too, in company with the "Jupiter," for no move was made that day.

On the following morning we were still moored there doing practically nothing. It was here that an extraordinary thing happened. There was a terrible tide running, and we nearly did the "Grecian Bend"! Our ship was moored on a three-quarter ebb tide, when all of a sudden she swung round stern up the river with both cables drawing —executing a complete right-about turn.

I have never seen such a thing in my life before, although I have anchored in most of the largest rivers in the world. Every one aboard was absolutely paralysed to see the ship turn in such a fashion, and so quickly that the anchors were dragged quite a lot. We had to get them up again and re-moor the ship farther ahead. This meant "in nets" again, and naturally cursing knew no bounds; we had our hands very full for the remainder of the day.

50 LAST CRUISE OF THE "MAJESTIC"

The next day the ship attempted another "Grecian Bend"—not so violent as the day before, but sufficient to convince the crew that something was wrong with the world. The weather got dirtier and dirtier, and bitterly cold into the bargain. To the night-watchers on the bridge with no shelter whatever it was terrible. Fortunately the Admiralty had risen to the occasion, and had provided watch-keepers with a rubber suit and sea-boots to keep out some of the cold; so there was certainly something to be thankful for.

On November 20th I and some others were detailed for a small vessel with Yeoman of Signals P. Lawton to relieve men going on pass belonging to H.M.S. "Victorious." The vessel belonged to the Humber Conservancy Board, and is used for signalling purposes. She was not a bad little boat, and particularly clean throughout.

There were four of the H.M.B. men on board, and four naval ratings—in all, a nice little party. Life went on very smoothly on board the vessel, but she proved a dirty little sea-boat whenever it began to blow, or when a bit of a swell got up. Her chief delight was to bury herself into the trough

ON A NEW MISSION

of the sea, which would break on board, and then when she rose again she took a positive delight in throwing the water all over herself and distributing shower-baths lavishly. But that was only a detail, after all. We were supplied with rations from the ship, but we had to cook them ourselves, which was a bit inconvenient, since the cooking appliances were, to say the least, primitive. However, we managed to rub along in quite a respectable fashion until December 11th, when we received orders to rejoin our ship again, as she was about to leave the Humber. The " Jupiter " had already left for an unknown northerly destination.

We waited about all day for an opportunity to leave the vessel, but the heavy seas made it impossible. Towards night, however, the picket-boat managed to get us away, and we bade farewell to all on board, including " Skimps," the great naval artist of the Fleet !

We arrived on board the " Majestic " after an exceedingly dirty journey, and endeavoured to find out whither we were bound; but, as usual, the whole thing was wrapped in mystery, and speculation was rife.

CHAPTER V

BOMBARDING THE BELGIAN COAST

WE were out of the Humber before four o'clock the next morning and were heading down south. The usual destroyer flotilla came to meet us, and informed us that they had instructions to escort us as far as Dover. On the way down we passed a considerable amount of wreckage, which I took to be the remains of the less fortunate ships that had fallen foul of the U-boats. Guns were manned day and night, but no inquiring submarine was good enough to show its nose to us.

It was blowing a gale from the S.W. by the time we entered the Channel, and we experienced considerable difficulty in tieing up the ship in Dover harbour; but the skilful handling of the ship by the captain, who was a most excellent seaman, finally got the job done.

BOMBARDING THE BELGIAN COAST

In the harbour we found H.M.S. "Revenge," the only battleship in commission older than the "Majestic." It was certainly an historic meeting of the good old "has beens," but nevertheless both ships looked as though they had a good deal of fight left in them. Towards night we learned our destination. We were to proceed in company with the "Revenge" for the purpose of bombarding the Belgian coast. Our hearts beat high at that most acceptable scrap of news, and in order to celebrate the great occasion the "bhoys" improvised a concert that night. The musical programme was more popular than classical, as might well be supposed, and the star turn of the evening was "Tanky's" effort, entitled, "Put a little Bit away for a Rainy Day," which brought the house down. It was the first time since mobilisation that I had heard a song on board ship, and I have no doubt the hilarity and general light-heartedness was due to the fact that we were really going to do something on the morrow.

In the morning the two "old horses" sallied forth, looking for likely prey, which failed to turn up. Of course we were escorted, which was only proper seeing that the days of our youth were past and our speed not all that could be desired. Anyhow, we got there eventually, and anchored for the night off Ostend.

The following day we made an early start up the coast with nets in and decks cleared for action. Near the shore were a pair of monitors blazing away at the enemy's positions, but we passed them and went farther up the coast with the "Revenge," which opened fire at 8 a.m. with her heavy guns at positions close inland. Apparently we were off Westend, but there was no means of ascertaining.

Our own bombardment, when we started, didn't last very long, as we learned that the enemy, having probably "got wind" of our object, had shifted farther inland. So we returned sorrowfully to Dover, feeling a sense of deep disappointment. It seemed very humiliating to have gone all that distance just for the purpose of slinging a few shells at nothing; but I suppose all these little things are sent to try us.

At Dover we learned that submarines had been sighted in the Channel. In the harbour we found the old "Montrose," of Crippen fame, getting fitted with apparatus to secure

BOMBARDING THE BELGIAN COAST 55

it against possible submarine attack. Some of our men were working aboard her, as labour was difficult to obtain on shore. However, all the labour that was being put into her proved to be in vain, for, just as she was being put into position a sudden gale sprang up from the S.W., and a gigantic sea swept right over the Pier and sent the " Montrose " staggering across to the eastern entrance, through which she escaped into the Channel, to be ultimately wrecked on the coast. Fortunately, there were no men on board her at the time.

Christmas Day proved to be a very drab and sober affair. A lot of the crew were ashore working on various jobs in the bit of a yard which they had there. There was no service of any kind aboard, so we beguiled the weary hours in a kind of sing-song and dreamed of the Christmases of yore, and those which we hoped the future held for us. A little excitement was occasioned by the arrival of a Taube which merely dropped a bomb on some poor man's cabbage-patch, and then scurried back across the Channel as fast as it possibly could.

During our stay at Dover another Taube paid us a visit, but the poor aviator must have suffered with defective vision, for he dropped his cargo bang into the sea, where I dare say there was plenty of room for it.

On the last day of the year we left Dover and proceeded down Channel once more to the usual "unknown destination." It was filthily dark, and a rather eerie prelude to the New Year. I dare say every one on board wondered where on earth they'd be on the next New Year's Eve, and it was good for the comfort of some that they didn't know.

Eight bells by the hand of a Royal Marine ushered in 1915, and, having done four hours' watch, I went below to "catch the bird," giving the customary season's greetings to the "relief" before doing so, and learning from them that our destination was Portland.

At 4 a.m. our progress was arrested by a message just as we were passing the Isle of Wight, which instructed us to go back to Portsmouth; we arrived there to hear that H.M.S. "Formidable" had been torpedoed just ahead of us down Channel. It had been a dirty night, and I guessed that the poor chaps would have little chance of

BOMBARDING THE BELGIAN COAST 57

being saved. Later I heard that the number rescued was comparatively small. God rest their souls! it's a vile end finishing in that way, without a chance to put up a fight.

We left Portland at 4.30 p.m. with a bit of wind blowing up from the S.W.; after clearing the Isle of Wight we began to feel the force of it. Our escort of T.B.D.'s were being washed down fore and aft, and the old " Majestic " shivered a bit as she shoved her nose into the swell. We kept our eyes well skinned for U-boats, for there wouldn't have been much chance for us in a sea like that. At last, after an eternity of suspense, the dawn broke, and we could see the T.B.D.'s rushing about like mad. Soon we saw Portland Hump loom up through the haze, and every one gave vent to a huge sigh of relief. The old war-horse wouldn't be so bad at an exchange of greetings in the form of shells, but at dodging torpedoes she was something less than a novice, for 12 knots is little better than a crawl, in whatever light you look at it.

At Portland we had a lot of " old ships " who informed us, to our delight, that seventy of the " Formidable " crew had been picked up by the Brixham trawler "Provident." I could imagine the depth of pride in the hearts of the people in that mother of fishing ports.

We remained at Portland until February 1st, and were fortunate enough to get a few hours' leave every week—usually Wednesday 1 to 7 p.m. Every place beyond Weymouth was out of bounds as time would not permit going farther afield—but some of the men went, nevertheless. Probably the resultant delights were out of all proportion to any possible punishment.

During our stay we played a few football matches, but we didn't shine at " footer," which was not to be wondered at, considering the Methuselahs which manned our ship. There was also a cutter's race between the R.F.R. and the R.N.R., which resulted in a complete walk-over for the R.N.R., who were for the main part Cornish and Devon fishermen, born with an oar in their hands.

We were all expecting leave towards the end of the month. Some reckoned it would be seven days, others thought five or six quite possible and reasonable. At any rate, four days was unanimously declared to be the very minimum. We got ourselves ready for that glorious time and dreamed of the bliss it contained. Alas! such is war! On the 30th our captain informed us there would be no " leave," and that we had sailing orders for February 1st.

Sic transit gloria mundi.

CHAPTER VI

EASTWARD BOUND

On February 1st we said good-bye to Portland, not without a certain amount of pleasure, for sailors invariably dislike the place, and are always glad to see the back of it. We proceeded to sea in company with H.M.S. "Irresistible," escorted by a number of T.B.D.'s and headed down Channel. Once clear of the Channel we made for Ushant, so we guessed we were bound south or east. When clear of the submarine area, the T.B.D.'s parted company and left us to ourselves, and it was with no small sense of relief that we watched them fading into the distance, for we felt that we were free from attack by the wily U-boats, and since we all knew that there was not a single German warship left on the high seas, the result was a feeling of security that we had not known since mobilisation. Nevertheless, a good look-out was always kept, for the sea is notorious for hurling little surprise packets at you.

Thence onward, the voyage proved uneventful, one day being very much like another and nothing happening to show that this was anything but a "joy cruise" in the good old days before the leash was broken.

It didn't take long for the news to get abroad that we were bound for Malta. One never knows how the thing leaks out, but it nearly always does, and it circulates with a speed that is truly marvellous. Since we were heading in that direction there was no reason to doubt that Malta was our destination—as it proved to be.

Crossing the Bay of Biscay we had a terrible time. I have crossed the Bay a score of times, but never have I seen it so violent as it was then. The good old ship was like a cork in a maelstrom. Water was coming in everywhere. It was like an incessant waterspout, pounding on the decks, forcing its way through every little crack and cranny. All the messes had to be shifted to the Bag Flats, as no one could live forward in such a deluge.

For four days we lived the life of a fish

inhabiting the under-seas rather than the surface. It made one think that even the elements were animated by the spirit of war, and that somehow man had offended the powers that be, and was suffering accordingly.

Every one was mighty glad to get out of it. The remainder of the voyage to Cap Trafalgar was not so bad, as the weather began to be less hostile. After entering the Gut of Gibraltar we came across a considerable number of patrol boats. To our surprise we did not call at Gibraltar, but proceeded straight to Malta.

Once we stopped to do a little heavy gun practice, the " Irresistible " towing our target, after which we reversed the operation. All the time the weather was improving, and when we arrived at Malta it was quite delightful.

What a change from the comparative drabness of northern climes! Here were colour and warmth. All the hues of the spectrum were flung broadcast to distribute themselves on hill and dale, in heaven and sea itself. This jewel of the Mediterranean had a beauty entirely its own. Life was very primitive, man was content to wrest from the soil his means of subsistence. All round the shores, small rocks studded the sea, and even on these were fishermen, sustained by the spoil that came to their nets. On the moss-grown summits of these rocks a few goats browsed and capered within the rather meagre limits of their refuge.

Grottos and caverns abounded in every direction, hollowed out of the cliffs by the constant drift of the sea, and in the island itself life was calm and uneventful, full of a placid peacefulness and in absolute keeping with the soft landscapes and primitive delights.

Malta had a history, too, dating back to some 1600 B.C., when it was colonised by the Phœnicians, who were dispossessed of it by the Greeks in 736 B.C. To the Greeks it was known as Melitus, but their sway over it was brought to a sudden end some 230 years later, when they were driven out of it by the Carthaginians. Down through the centuries it changed hands constantly, from Roman to Goth, from Arab to Turk, until in 1814 it became part of the British Empire, in which proud estate let us hope it will always remain.

When we arrived there on that glorious

February morning there were a lot of British and French warships, and by the unusual amount of activity it was obvious that something was in the wind, but what it might be I hadn't the vaguest notion.

On February 11th we coaled ship and the following day she was taken into dry dock to have her bottom cleaned and painted, and her under-water fittings overhauled. In the afternoon I went ashore and found the place thronged with French and British sailors. Everywhere there was dancing and singing, and the usual manifestations of joy. I doubt not that Malta had never seen such a gathering of humanity in her streets. All her varied history could present nothing like this. French chansons and English music-hall airs mingled with each other, and both nations apparently strove to outdo each other in hilarity. Very soon I found out what this huge collection of men and ships signified. *The Fleet was going to attempt to run the Dardanelles!*

That, indeed, was something like news. I had a set opinion on that particular operation, but it isn't for a sailor to venture opinions for or against, and I was delighted at the thoughts of being in something big.

EASTWARD BOUND

The next few days I spent in visiting all the chief places of interest. The Chapel on Bones was certainly rather a gruesome place, ornamented by no less than 2,000 skulls, and set off by the inclusion of a fair quantity of bones and skeletons. There were also the skeletons of two ladies who perished when Napoleon conquered the island over a century ago. I paid a visit to the Citta Vecchia, seven miles out, and exactly opposite the bay where St. Peter was wrecked. Here there is a magnificent cathedral named St. Paul and St. Peter, full of fine pictures and furnished with exquisite mosaic flooring. The rather extensive catacombs were well worth a visit, for it was here that St. Paul is supposed to have lived for a time after his shipwreck.

Returning to Valetta, I found a fancy dress carnival in full swing. It was, of course, the annual carnival which takes place just before Lent begins. It had, I was told, been organised on a modest scale this year owing to the war, but nevertheless it was an imposing spectacle, and well attended.

In the dock alongside us was the French battleship "Jean Bart," which had been torpedoed in the Adriatic about Christmas time. She had, however, managed to keep afloat, and to make Malta with all aboard her safe. They were now busy patching her up, which she sorely needed, for the torpedo had taken about 40 feet off her keel at the bows, and had blown away part of her stem-post.

Work on the "Majestic" was proceeding at great speed, and a few days would see her ready for sea again. As a kind of extra embellishment, they fitted a mine-bumper over our bows, and if its efficiency were in anything like proportion to its complicatedness we could well afford to laugh at mines.

Every afternoon I managed to get ashore, and every day I found the air more vibrant with war news and rumours. The "Ark Royal" arrived with her swarm of waterplanes, and British and French mine-sweepers, and miscellaneous craft steamed in without cessation.

Never in her palmiest days had Malta aspired to such importance. No doubt it presented gay sights in those old days when Greeks and Carthaginians swarmed round the old rock in their wooden ships, and waged mighty battles with short swords, spears, arrows, and what not; but nothing like this. Here was immense power sitting silently on the blue waters—conserved energy that, at the word, could belch fire and death unending. Could one of those old Greeks have seen the sight and witnessed the devastating effect of but one large-calibre, high explosive shell, he would have slunk back to his tomb with quaking fear in his soul. And yet it might have been a pageant, so calmly and orderly it lay. It might have been a peace mission whose object was to spread abroad good fellowship and love among men, did not the conscience whisper its real import. Somewhere farther eastward, hundreds of good fellows in the full glory of their youth were to be swept to eternity by the fates which attend war. Some of those mighty ships, magnificent in their strength, would never return to harbour. Yet they lay there, beautiful in the southern colouring, and men came and went from them in boats, happy at heart, with the lilt of a song in their lips, each secure in the thought that he, at least, would return. For that is the way of youth, buoyed up with a sense of immortality, feeling that Death may come and take his toll—a brother, a comrade, but not *them*, that were an impossibility. The feeling is always there, even when things are at their blackest, and lives go out like candle-flames. It is the egotism of youth, that surmounts all danger. Call it courage, bravery, anything you like, but in reality it is nothing less than the inherent, perhaps unconscious egotism at the heart of each healthy man.

It seemed strange to reflect that a little over a century ago, on this very spot, General Vaubois surrendered to General Pigot, who commanded the British and allied forces, and yet here were French and British sailors arm in arm, and the ships of both navies floating side by side in the bay, each outvieing the other in their zest to meet the common enemy.

On February 21st we came out of dock, and passed down the grand harbour to sea. What a farewell! Every place of vantage was crowded with people, and a great burst of cheering went up from every point. From the town came the pealing of bells, which reverberated over the water with a strange beauty, and somehow made me think of England and the streets of my own native town.

CHAPTER VII

THE DARDANELLES

WE churned along in a northerly direction under a glorious sky with a sun that struck pleasantly warm. Early the next day we fell in with nine French mine-sweepers, some of which were of a very small type. They were all bound for the Dardanelles, so we stood by them as the weather was freshening a bit, and a nasty sea was " getting up."

The next morning we put into a sheltered place called Idaho, to the west of Cape Matapan, and remained there until 3 p.m.; but, as the sea showed no sign of abating, we left the mine-sweepers to make the best way they could, later on, and promised to report them on our arrival at the Dardanelles.

Later on in the day we received the news that we should meet the fleet in the morning at a certain rendezvous. Fortunately we enjoyed a good night, as the weather began to ease up, and early next morning we fell in with part of the fleet. We joined up with them and made the island of Tenedos, which lies about twelve miles from the entrance of the Straits.

On our arrival (February 25th) we found a whole lot of French and British warships standing by.

Over at the entrance of the Straits the fleet had already commenced bombarding the six outer forts—three on the European side and three on the Asiatic side—and, as the day was clear, we had a fairly good view of the operations.

The "Queen Elizabeth," "Lord Nelson," and "Agamemnon" opened fire from a long range, and apparently soon began to put the forts out of action. It was impossible to see the effect on the forts themselves, as they were obscured from us by tremendous clouds of dust and smoke; but, since the ships began to creep nearer and nearer, it was pretty certain that they were meeting with little opposition.

The big new ships kept well away, but the older vessels continued their approach, and at close range opened up broadsides time after time. It must have been hell inside those forts with shells raining in upon them every second; but I have no doubt they were vacated the moment that "Lizzie's" giant "birthday gifts" began to arrive.

At 6 p.m. the bombarding ships returned for the night, and we learned that all the forts at the entrance had been silenced. Not one of the ships had been touched at all, so that the honours of the day fell wholly to us. In the morning we got under way in company with H.M.S. "Albion" and some destroyers and mine-sweepers—both French and British—and proceeded towards the Straits. Our orders were to destroy the bridge at the back of the Kum Kale Forts.

It didn't take us long to get across that bit of water. We prepared for action on the way over, which is not saying much, for a warship is nearly always ready for action, except for a few minor details. We had breakfast pretty well as usual, but cleared up a little more quickly, so that we might be assured that everything was in order—deadlights closed in case of fire, fire-hoses connected and running—for the deck is kept flooded when in action.

At 9 a.m. "Action" was sounded, and

away we went to quarters; being a signalman, my place was on deck by the flags. The mine-sweepers led the way until we reached the entrance of the Straits, and then we took over the lead, ploughing our way proudly up the narrow channel.

What a triumph for the "Majestic," to be the first ship to enter the Straits; at her age, too! At 9.15 we opened fire on the bridge with 6-inch shells, and soon had the thing scattered to oblivion. It was then we discovered a party of Turkish troops round about the ruins of the forts. Poor devils!—a few shrapnel shells literally blew them off the earth. The few that escaped scuttled like rabbits among the broken masonry and general wreckage.

We proceeded slowly up the Straits, opening fire on various places that might possibly conceal troops or batteries. For a time we did as we liked, but as we made progress we gradually came under the fire of Turkish batteries. Now and again would come a flash from behind a hill, and then the dull "wooff" of the shell as it struck the land behind us or exploded on contact with the sea. Sometimes the impact with the water was not enough to detonate the shell—

THE DARDANELLES

dependent upon the style of fuse mechanism, I suppose—and all that happened was a sudden perpendicular jet of water. The real excitement came when the first enemy shell found its target, and the old ship quivered with the explosion. That ought to have been sufficient to keep every one below except those whose duty compelled them to remain on deck, but it had precisely the opposite effect. Every man who was not on duty scampered up to see the "fun"; most of them seemed to regard it as a kind of regatta, and the captain repeatedly had to order them below. But still they crept up, filled with an insatiable curiosity.

It was the first time that any of them had been under fire, and their first natural impulse was to see just what was happening. I reckoned that as soon as a few men had been killed, the novelty of it would quickly wear off, and there would be very little unnecessary exposure in the future.

In all we penetrated the Straits to a distance of five miles, pounding away like mad the whole time, and miraculously missing the hail of shells which was rained at us. In all we were hit four times, but the shots were small and the damage was negligible. Best of all, there was not a single casualty on our side, so it was argued that the old "war-horse" had acquitted herself nobly. We arrived back at Tenedos late in the afternoon and anchored for the night.

The next day (February 27th) we remained at anchor until 8 p.m. and then got under way to relieve ships patrolling the mouth of the Straits. It was here that I had a bit of an accident which fortunately had little or no effects. I was going on watch when the syren commenced blowing off, owing to the wire having caught under a rung of the iron ladder leading to the fore-top. I went up to clear it, and was just doing so when my foot slipped and down I came a full twenty-five feet on my back. I was just beginning to wonder, in a dazed fashion, how many ribs I had broken and how long I should be in hospital, when the doctor came, and to my utter amazement told me that I was quite intact and that nothing was broken at all! I had to go bed for the night instead of on watch, but, beyond a painful stiffness the next morning, I was fit as ever.

The next day was Sunday, and a wretched

THE DARDANELLES 75

Sabbath it was. The weather had turned positively filthy, so we contented ourselves with patrolling up and down outside the Straits—a most monotonous and thankless task.

After a very quiet night we started work in earnest the next morning. The Turks were certainly wasting no time, and were observed to be placing some field batteries into position on shore. Off we went to expostulate in the best practical fashion. All day we pounded away at them, and I dare say caused them no little inconvenience, but the actual damage could not be ascertained. We were subjected to a pretty stiff fire all the time, but luck was with us and we came home for the night unscathed.

Things went rather tamely with us until March 4th, when we were detailed with five other ships to effect a landing at Seddul Bahr, on the Dardanelles side of the village. The landing party consisted of a number of R.M.L.I. from the various ships, and a few from one of the troop-ships which had arrived, together with about 2,000 Marines, making a total of about 4,000 in all.

The party was put off from the ships in ship-boats, towed by steamers which were armed with maxim guns and light Q.F. guns in the bows.

Nothing happened until the boat was within about 300 yards of the beach, and then Abdul opened up a fusillade of fire from various points in the hills, and from the village itself. It was splendid to see the way the men received their " baptism." Every one was perfectly cool and collected. A man dropped here and there, but still the boats went on in a cool, methodical sort of way. Luckily it was only rifle fire; had the Turks been armed with a few field-guns or light Q.F.'s there would have been few of our landing-party left to tell the tale.

On reaching the beach there was a bit of a scuffle, the Turks desperately resisting our attempts to land. Eventually they retired to the cliffs, keeping up a continuous fire from good cover.

The landing-party made an attempt to get to the village, but it was too weak to overcome the opposition, for hundreds of Turks had come in from over the hills to reinforce their defence, and the Marines were exposed to fire from every quarter without much chance of retaliating, as isolated rifle-fire can seldom be located.

THE DARDANELLES

The ships came to the rescue and began to deluge the hills with shrapnel, but though the damage done was undoubtedly great, the advantage was always with the enemy, and to have continued the advance in the face of circumstances would have been madness, so the landing-party reluctantly re-embarked and returned to the ships.

For a time, however, the ships' guns continued "searching" the hills, and I can vouch for some execution, for we were fortunate enough to catch a large party of Turks in a ravine, where they got it hot from both common and shrapnel shell. There was no means of escape for them, and we could see the flying fragments of the shells strike in every direction, thinning their ranks until they withered away.

We didn't get off scot-free though; a 5-inch shell from the Asiatic shore hit the "Majestic" about the starboard after-gangway, went through to the paymaster's cabin, which it completely wrecked, in addition to damaging the cabins on either side of it, and ended by setting the place on fire.

The career of that shell was extraordinary. It came in on the starboard side, went through the cabin, across the deck, smashing a ladder in its flight, bounced off the side of the turret, took the top of the rail leading down below, hit a beam overhead on the port side, threw a heap of splinters into the wardroom pantry, which cut open the steward's head, and then finished its course on the deck below, where a large piece of it was pounced upon by a signalman. All that fuss, and not one casualty beyond the steward's broken head! I learned that the casualties among the landing-party were small considering the circumstances—29 killed and 50 wounded, exclusive of a few casualties among the boats' crews.

We withdrew outside the Straits, did a little patrolling for the night, and were released early next morning, upon which we steamed to Tenedos and anchored for the rest of the day.

On the 6th we made an early start for the Dardanelles, and it promised to be an interesting day, for we learned that we were to go right up to Chanak, and carry out a bombardment there. Chanak is twelve miles from the entrance, and marks the beginning of the "Narrows," so it would be foolish to expect anything in the nature of a picnic.

THE DARDANELLES

At 9 a.m. "Action" was sounded, and off we went full steam ahead with three other ships to keep us company. All the way we kept up a sort of running fire. The ships followed each other at intervals of about one mile, this formation being adopted in order that the following ship could take the fire of the Turkish batteries, while the ship ahead turned to come down again. It was a thrilling sight to watch the ships ahead dodging the fire. Great shells would fall all round them, throwing up huge fountains of water and smothering the ships. The firing at that time was atrociously bad ; with anything like moderate gun-fire the ships would have been riddled. We made six runs up in all, doing good work with our guns and escaping as though by a miracle. At times it was perfect hell, shells screaming over head, and sending up the water right under our bows, while the air shook with the cannonade.

Before we finished we had a real shock. There was a great explosion and the ship shook fore and aft. Every one was on the alert to find out what had happened. We were soon relieved from our anxiety. We had been badly struck on the port after battery door and quarter-deck. Such a pot-mess I have never seen before. The quarter-deck was ripped to ribbons; the battery door had been blown along the upper deck. The after bulk-head, where the shell had exploded, was a regular "curiosity" for the heat and force from the explosion had caused the metal to run down like treacle. Everything in the vicinity was smashed to atoms—and yet there was not one casualty! In truth, we began to think that the old "Majestic" was charmed.

The same night we went up again to cover the mine-sweepers at their dangerous work. Theirs was a most risky job, for they were under fire the whole time. No praise could be too great for the courage of their crews, who worked with magnificent coolness under a hot fire. All night we stayed with them, and on the following day—Sunday—had a brief respite. But the work still went on. The French went right up the Straits, performing a similar task to that undertaken by us on the previous day. Only one ship was hit—damage unknown.

The next day we proceeded to Mudros in the island of Lemnos, where we arrived at 8 a.m. There was quite a fine harbour there, and to our surprise it was choked full of troopships and merchant vessels of all classes from tramp collier to the largest liners afloat. This was my first trip to Mudros, and I took a liking to the place immediately. The harbour was sheltered, being fairly land-locked with high hills all round. The more I saw of the place the better I liked it. We got fruit and eggs from the natives which was a pleasant change from our usual fare. Tobacco was also grown on the island, but I never tried any of it. In former times the island was renowned for its celebrated Lemnian earth, which was exported in large quantities.

We coaled the ship, replenished the magazines with ammunition, and then, to our great joy, stayed there the whole night, enjoying a good long sleep in our hammocks.

The following day we cleaned ship and put to sea at 1.30 p.m. Arrived in the Dardanelles, we went on patrol duty for the night; but things were very quiet, so we continued our patrolling through the next day. Now and again we would fire a few rounds at some suspicious object on shore, but it was doubtful if any good came of it. That part of the land seemed to be deserted.

For the next few days we continued patrolling, but there was great work done by the mine-sweepers. Volunteers were called from all ships, and I am glad to say that the "Majestic" gave her full quota. We supplied the picket-boat with crews for several of those little ventures in connection with the mine-sweeping operations. There was nothing in the whole business to equal these little excursions in hair-raising thrills. The boats had to go right up into the entrance of the Narrows, where the enemy's searchlights played full on them, and the Turkish batteries were free to hurl lead and death at them to their hearts' content.

It was a marvel to me that any of us ever got back alive, and yet we did, as witness this diary. Fortunately at such moments the excitement overleaps the sense of danger, and only afterwards does one get the picture in its true perspective. All the men's names were called for and noted, so I suppose it was considered a bit of a feat.

I learned later that while the "Amethyst" was covering the mine-sweepers and picket-boats, she got badly holed, a shell entering the stoker's bath-room just as the watch was coming off duty. It exploded there, killing practically every one of them. Other shells had also struck her, but none with such terrible results.

In the evening a destroyer went alongside her and took off twenty-four dead for burial at sea. These sights are always touching. The mere knowledge that casualties have occurred does not affect the emotions in any large degree, for one naturally expects them; but when the ceremonials are performed and one sees a T.B.D. steaming to sea with her quarter-deck covered with Union Jacks, and realises that sewn up in the canvas are twenty-four dear comrades who yesterday were alive and well, a certain moistness will inevitably spring to the eyes, no matter how hardened you may have become.

That night the mine-sweepers again suffered, many of them falling victims to the growing effectiveness of the enemy's fire.

We coaled ship next day, and in the evening welcomed the arrival of a Russian cruiser called "Askold." She was a business-looking cruiser, no doubt, but it didn't take the "bhoys" long to find a nickname for her. She was christened the "Packet of

Woodbines," on account of her possessing five funnels.

For two days we were kept at patrol work, until March 16th, when we steamed to Tenedos and dropped anchor at 8 p.m.

CHAPTER VIII

THE GENERAL BOMBARDMENT

No sooner were we at anchor than great news began to circulate. The gist of it was, that on the morrow there was to be a general bombardment of the Dardanelles. Certainly all things pointed to its being correct, for all flag-officers and captains were ordered on board the Flagship, and gunnery officers and captains of guns called below, where they were given a lecture on how the action was to be carried out.

It looked as though things were coming to a head at last. At any rate, another twenty-four hours would give us a pretty good idea as to what was really happening.

It didn't take long for the news to become common property, and to be sufficiently confirmed to remove any doubts on the matter. Excitement grew apace, and the pros and cons of the operation were discussed in every hole and corner. We had learned by this time to call the Narrows the " Mouth of Hell," and they were invariably referred to as such. Most men seemed to think we could get through the Mouth of Hell all right, but what was to happen after that no one had the faintest notion. It was pretty certain there would be no return ticket to Chanak, and, since we should be obliged to go right on to Constantinople, several men notified their intention, with a grin, of applying for four days' leave.

The argument developed on quite serious lines. How far could we get beyond the Narrows ? Could we ever get back again ? What was the use of going up when we hadn't troops to clear and hold the mainland ? If we got right up and allowed the Turks to mount big guns along the Straits in our own rear, how could we ever hope to get back again ?

It was certainly a knotty problem, but all were unanimously agreed that things would hum on the morrow.

I give here a list of the ships which were to take part in the historic event.

First our flagship " Queen Elizabeth." Then the Dreadnought cruiser "Inflexible," pre-Dreadnoughts "Agamemnon" and "Lord Nelson"; battleships "Queen," "London," "Prince of Wales," "Implacable," and "Cornwallis," these practically all in one class from 1900 down. Then "Swiftsure" and "Triumph," both purchased from the Chilian Government during the Russo-Japanese War. Then, in order of age, "Albion," "Canopus," "Vengeance," "Prince George," "Ocean," "Irresistible," "Goliath," and last, but not least, the old grandfather of the battle-fleet, the "Majestic."

We were utterly outdone in age by the French battleships. These were "Charlemagne," "Bouvet," "Gaulois," "Sufferin," "Henry IV," and "Jaurequiberry," this last having attained an age of twenty-three years. Then followed a string of cruisers: "Bacchante," "Euryalus," "Talbot," "Doris," "Dublin," "Dartmouth," "Minerva," and "Amethyst," with the Russian cruiser "Askold" bringing up the rear.

Following the Armada were T.B.D.'s, torpedo craft, submarines, mine-sweepers, repair ships and small craft too numerous to detail.

The morrow dawned and with it was born a great surprise. Very soon we learned that there would be no bombardment that day. The news was staggering. Every one was asking what had happened. It eventually became known that the Admiral was leaving for home !

On the mess deck there was a perfect fire of comment. The Irish members were particularly disappointed, for the Admiral was an Irishman, and to-day was St. Patrick's Day. What an honour to Old Erin it would have been !

We choked down our sorrow, and awaited further events. During the day H.M.S. " Phaeton " arrived, bringing Sir Ian Hamilton, who had apparently been sent out from England.

After the departure of the Admiral Carden Admiral De Robeck hoisted his flag in command of the fleet, and we heard that the bombardment would commence the following morning on lines as previously arranged.

That put a different expression on every one's face. After all, one day didn't make much difference. Little did we think, when patrolling up and down the Channel from the Wolf Light to Start Bay, that we should participate in such an operation as this. In those days we used to envy the men in

THE GENERAL BOMBARDMENT

the North Sea! and now their work seemed positively tame compared with the task that lay before us. The prospects seemed like meat and drink to the crew—every one was so shockingly polite and nice-tempered. They were all so keen to prove that the old "Majestic" still had a good punch left in her.

During the day all boats were sent away from the ships with the exception of one cutter, since it would be dangerous to keep boats on board on account of fire. Also there would be the likelihood of flying splinters which might cause injuries. Rations were served out for the next day so that the cooks could get the dinners cooked overnight, as all galley-fires must be out before going into action. We signalmen get our flags ready on the upper deck in canvas haversacks outside the foremost 6-inch gun casement, this being the only favourable spot. The position was a little exposed, but it could not be helped in those old-pattern ships.

Everything now appeared to be in readiness for the fray. Our beloved Padre had not overlooked his part, and had arranged for a communion service early in the morning.

The evening passed off quietly, the gunnery officer once more giving a lecture on how the ships were to form up and come into action.

The following is, as near as I can recollect, the position of the ships.

First Line : " Agamemnon," "Lord Nelson," " Queen Elizabeth," "Inflexible"; wing ships, " Swiftsure " and " Triumph."

Second Line : " Charlemagne," " Sufferin," " Gaulois," " Bouvet."

Third Line : " Queen," " London," " Prince of Wales," " Implacable;" Wing ships, " Majestic " and " Ocean."

Fourth Line : "Canopus," "Prince George," " Irresistible," and " Goliath."

In addition to these there were T.B.D.'s, etc., etc., in case of accident. The position of the ships may not be correct in every detail, but that was the formation planned for the attack. Each line as it advanced to a certain spot was to turn outwards and form behind the next line astern to support it, and so with the next line until all four lines had been to the front.

The great morning arrived, and at 7.30 the First Line of the Fleet was preparing to

THE GENERAL BOMBARDMENT 91

form up with the French ships, already formed, waiting to fall in behind them. On such occasions one pays no attention to time —it ceases to be as far as we are concerned. In a very short time breakfast was over, and we were heading for the Straits.

The Padre had finished his service, which I am pleased to say was very well attended, both by officers and men, and everything was ready down to the clearing of all stools and tables. The sick quarters were removed to the flats, and hose-pipes were connected as usual.

Very soon the boom of the big guns of the First Line told us that "action" had commenced. We were then about three miles from the entrance, and steaming at ten knots. As we approached closer we could see great spurts of water flung up all round the First Line ships, which were well away up the Straits—about six miles by this time. The roar of the guns was deafening—there seemed to be no interval of silence, nothing but a continuous, nerve-shattering noise, that rocked the atmosphere and turned the world in which we moved into pandemonium.

The First Line was now manœuvring outwards from the centre to fall in rear of the French line. The French ships advanced, keeping up a terrific fire with enemy's shells pulverising the water all round them. Suddenly an awful explosion was heard, and for a moment the whole place seemed blotted out of existence. When visibility was once more possible, we saw that the " Inflexible " had had an accident of some kind. She was out of action, and was steaming low down in the water, while her fighting top was damaged. But that made no difference to the action, it went on ding-dong, more furious than ever. The French ships of the Second Line were still advancing, keeping up an incessant fire all the time. By this time we were right in the fighting zone, and catching it hot from all quarters. Shells were screaming overhead in a terrifying, vicious kind of way, and occasionally one would land on the ship ; but no serious damage was done.

We were getting nearer and nearer to the " Mouth of Hell," and the nearer we got the more we realised how apt was the name we had adopted. It was veritable hell, with belching flame and smoke, and noises that made the day hideous. Through all this

THE GENERAL BOMBARDMENT 93

flame-lit inferno the ships crept with the very water boiling with rage.

The French ships were retiring to the rear and the Third Line was moving up to the front when the first disaster occurred. They had just turned out of the line, with the "Gaulois" leading, and were heading down stream, when suddenly up went a great jet of water around the "Gaulois," which had apparently struck a floating mine. She proceeded all safe as far as we could see, but a few minutes after the "Bouvet," which was following, had a similar experience; but, alas! with fatal results. She heeled over, toppled completely, and within three minutes was lying at the bottom of the Dardanelles. The swiftness of it was staggering, and the loss of life must have been enormous, for there was no time for the men to attempt to save themselves, with the exception of a few that remained above deck, and some of these were picked up by one of the ship's picket-boats, over on the right wing.

From where I stood, it looked as though there was an internal explosion—a magazine or a boiler; but the place was one infernal din, and it was impossible to identify any one sound.

Our line was now leading the attack, with the Fourth Line following behind. In rear of the Fourth Line were the "Queen Elizabeth," "Lord Nelson," and "Agamemnon." The "Inflexible" had retired out of sight, also the French line; thus fifteen ships remained in action.

Imagine the sight! Our own line blazing away like mad, the enemy's shells coming from all directions, and bursting on every side, and then, to supplement this, our original First Line firing over us from the rear. It was one raging hurricane of fire which never slackened, but rather increased in intensity.

We relieved our wing ship, which began to drop astern, and continued the advance. The Narrows were looming up ahead of us, through the fog of battle, but we weren't there yet. Another magazine went up with a terrific explosion, audible even above the roar of the combat. Chanak seemed to be in flames, judging by the huge cloud of smoke that towered above it.

It was impossible to judge time, when every second was crowded with action and excitement; but some one said it was 3 p.m., which meant that we had been in the furnace

THE GENERAL BOMBARDMENT 95

for three hours. We hadn't to wait long before our second disaster occurred. Away on the right the " Irresistible " struck a floating mine and began to sink fast. Thank God! it wasn't a second " Bouvet," for she was able to move, and made for shore down stream, in order to evade the enemy's fire. She didn't get far, though. Either she struck ground or the water had got into the stokehold or engine-room. Immediately up went the signals for the T.B.D.'s to come and take off the crew. I shall never forget the sight of the T.B.D.'s rushing like mad to their work of mercy. The " Irresistible " had now become the special mark of the Turkish batteries. Every gun they could muster was brought to bear on her, and at times she was blotted out of sight by the deluge of spray which the shells made as they entered the water around her.

By the time the T.B.D.'s got alongside, the Turks had got the range, but the " angels of the fleet " seemed to laugh at the cannonade and get the crew off with amazing quickness, with the exception of a few who remained on the ship. Thank God! the work of rescue was carried out with small damage and very few casualties.

In the meantime the fleet was raining shells on the Turkish batteries. The "Irresistible" seemed to be making a brave fight to keep afloat, but she was sinking slowly but surely. The "Ocean" then went to her assistance, but apparently finding the case hopeless, came away clear of her again.

Another calamity! No sooner did the "Ocean" get away than she struck a floating mine and heeled over. We held our breath and waited for her to disappear; still she floated, with 12 feet of her bottom sticking out of the water. Up went the signals again, and down came the T.B.D.'s churning the water into foam in the anxiety to get there in time. We craned our necks to watch this race with death, for the T.B.D.'s were three miles down the Straits at that moment.

The Turks were letting the "Ocean" have it for all they were worth. Shells struck her everywhere. Forward she was an absolute wreck, and she was sinking fast. We looked towards the "Irresistible," which was still floating, and saw that some of her guns were in action—now and again smoke and fire would belch forth from the muzzles.

The T.B.D.'s were close up to the "Ocean" now, and soon commenced their work of

THE GENERAL BOMBARDMENT 97

taking off the crew under terrific fire. There appeared to be a big battery round one of the points which we were unable to get at from our position, so our captain decided to go farther up in order to engage it.

Off we went, too dazed and maddened by the indescribable conditions to care what happened. Once round the point, we saw our quarry and opened upon it quickly. Before long we were rewarded by seeing a great explosion right over the battery, and concluded that a magazine had blown up.

We were now well up ahead of the remainder of the fleet, and some one was telling me that it was 4.30, when we had a terrible shaking up. A salvo of big stuff caught us on the port side, just before the battery door, and at the same time our fighting top was knocked to pieces. The bridge was in a shocking mess, and the stays of the mast all gone. Down below it was perfect hell. The hydraulic pipes had all burst, and water and steam were escaping in every direction. One shell that exploded in the forecastle sent pieces smashing through the bulkhead and battery doors forward, wounding nine men who happened to be in the gangway at the time.

As for myself, I have a lot to thank Providence for. My throat was parched through the smoke and heat, and I got relieved for a few minutes to get a drink of water. When I got back the poor fellow who relieved me had got both his legs smashed, and several pieces of shell in various parts of his body.

The captain, too, had a narrow escape. He had scarcely left the bridge when it was swept fore and aft. Had he stayed there a minute longer nothing could have saved him from violent injury or death.

Out of the nine wounded men, only one died, so that, everything considered, we had a great deal to be thankful for.

After this we retired a little astern, for it was obvious that we should not get through the Narrows that night, despite the fact that the Turkish fire was slackening considerably.

In the distance Chanak was like a great furnace, a huge red mass that threw a ghostly glare over the whole sky. The " Irresistible " and " Ocean " were still afloat, but it seemed as though their last fight had been fought. I saw the " Ocean " launched at Devonport dockyard, and met her again during the Boxer rising, but little did I dream, then, that we should meet again in such his-

THE GENERAL BOMBARDMENT 99

toric and altogether unimaginable circumstances.

Soon the light began to fail, rendering things more weird and awful than ever. We could see the leap of flame now from the muzzles of the Turkish guns under the high cliffs, and red-tinged smoke whirling away like grim and horrible spectres. The other ships were dropping away to the rear, but we still clung on for a time, all on our own, with the exception of the "Triumph," which was well in under the land over to the right.

There was little more to be done, as darkness was setting in (6.30 p.m.), so we were ordered to retire, which we did, thanking God we were still alive.

Once outside the Straits we found that the "Gaulois" had been run ashore on "Rabbit Island" to prevent her from sinking; but it turned out that she wasn't so badly holed, after all, and they would doubtless soon put her right again.

Arrived at Tenedos, we found the "Inflexible" close in shore with a host of salvage boats and other craft around her. She had also struck a mine and was severely damaged, but not beyond repair.

What a day! The myriad mental photographs which are made on such occasions are sufficient to last a man a life-time. I shall never forget the heroic little picket-boats rushing to the rescue of the few survivors of the "Bouvet," a tiny cockle-shell of a thing tearing into the teeth of that inferno with no thought save one, and that the noblest man can conceive.

And the signal-boys! It makes one burn with pride to think of them. All day they had to stand by the halliards with no cover over-head and very little anywhere else. I can see them now, squatting on a box of 12-pounder ammunition, smoking cigarettes to their hearts' content. A couple of them were a bit scared at first—as indeed were all of us—but they soon got over that, and cheerfully reconciled the situation. All were less than eighteen years of age, and yet they stood by patiently hour after hour and watched death stalk around in its most noisy and terrifying form.

We heard that, while we were up bombarding, a landing-party had landed at the entrance and demolished the guns that were left in the Forts—*and not a single Turk was seen*.

What a chance for an army! It could

have landed anywhere it liked without the slightest opposition.

We were soon at anchor, and, after clearing the decks a bit, piped down for sleep, wondering what the morrow would bring.

CHAPTER IX

AFTER THE BOMBARDMENT

THE next day (March 19th) there was no action, so we remained at anchor to clear away wreckage, and get on with the work of repairing ship. We had in all eleven pairs of signal halliards shot away, but we could not replace these until the rigging party had been aloft and repaired the stays and lifts of the mast and yards, many of which had been damaged and some shot clean away.

The lower fighting-top looked a pitiful wreck. Thank God! no man was in the top when it was struck. The carpenter's staff were busy as ants on the forecastle, and patching up the holes in the ship's side and deck, where the big hit had occurred. The deck was ripped up for a distance of twelve feet long by six feet wide, and the hole in the ship's side was approximately the same size. The shell that came through the side struck just abaft the sick-bay, and blew away the bulkhead. Again we were fortunate in having no one in there. Truly we seemed to have been specially favoured by providence.

The "Inflexible" was still close in-shore, though not actually beached. She had been struck in the submerge flat or torpedo-room, and had a few men there when it happened. I have no doubt they were drowned, as they would have stayed to do their duty, which was to close the escape-hatch.

I could get no news of the "Ocean" and the "Irresistible," but learned that the "Gaulois" was still on Rabbit Island, where she had been beached, and the crew taken off; but, since they were soon allowed to return to her, I assumed she was not in such a bad condition after all.

Work progressed with amazing speed. The rigging party soon had the yards and lifts mended, so up we went and got our new halliards rove and ready for action again.

The remains of the fleet also lay around us patching up and making themselves fit for the next attack. Some of the ships were coaling and taking in ammunition and shot.

All round were the signs of toil, men in the rigging, on the deck, over the sides, men everywhere armed with hammer and saw and chisel, untiring in their zest to put things ship-shape.

The scores of ships lying in that peaceful harbour, with sunlit hills towering on either side, presented a strange contrast to the scenes and events of the previous day. Even the bumboat was about, laden with edible produce of every description—eggs, figs, oranges, and fish, mixed up with cigarettes and various oddments, to say nothing of a couple of live chickens which made frantic attempts to escape. But money was short then, and the bumboat man had a slightly exaggerated idea of the worth of his wares, so we passed him by and left him to bleed other and perhaps more worldly-blessed victims.

Another day was spent in repairs, and in cleaning up ship. In the afternoon about forty men from the "Ocean" were transferred to us. From them we learned that both the "Ocean" and the "Irresistible" had gone to the bottom. Fortunately only one man was known to be missing from the "Ocean" and very few from the "Irresistible."

They all had pitiful tales to tell. Their forecastle had been smashed in and all the cat davids and anchors had fallen through to the mess below. When they had left the ship all her side forward was like a concertina. Most of the men had had miraculous escapes, but they thought less of that than of the pitiful sight that their dear old ship had presented. Most of them were R.N.R.'s from Brixham, and, as many of our men hailed from the same place, it was something like a family gathering.

In the afternoon the "Gaulois" was floated off the beach quite safely, which afforded us no little pleasure, for a ship saved is a ship gained.

The next morning the ammunition ship came alongside, and we took in a supply of "cannon fodder," a quantity which would make any ordinary man gasp, for the appetite of a gun is extraordinary. Later the weather turned very bad, a pretty fresh gale blowing down from the northland. We soon got orders to up anchor and proceed to the other side of the island for shelter, and, to our surprise and joy the "Inflexible" accompanied us round, to prove that she was getting fit again.

Arrived on the other side, we anchored and remained there for the night. The work of the carpenters, blacksmiths, etc., was marvellous. Everything was finished off neatly with touches of paint here and there to set it in harmony. At 4 p.m. we got under way again and proceeded to patrol the entrance of the Straits. Everything on shore seemed very quiet, but no doubt they were waiting for us to have another slap at them.

For the next few days nothing of any importance happened—with the exception that I was able to strike a bargain with the steward for a 14-lb tin of Irish butter, which was in the nature of a godsend, for we rarely got anything outside salt junk and hard biscuits; potatoes were things of the past—we hadn't seen one since Lord knows when!

Mine-sweeping was still carried on regularly, and we went out at intervals covering the mine-sweepers and doing general patrol work; but Abdul seemed to have vanished into thin air—although doubtless he was very much there even if not in evidence.

On April 1st we went off on an expedition in company with the "Swiftsure" and

AFTER THE BOMBARDMENT 107

"Minerva" and some destroyers and French mine-sweepers, to the Gulf of Adramystic, near the island of Mytilene.

We proceeded to the head of the gulf, and gazed with delight at the scene which lay before us. It was like some great inland lake, shimmering in the glorious sunlight, with scarcely a ripple on the water. It reminded me very much of the inland seas of Japan, wooded right down to the water's edge, with a colour scheme that changed as you watched. It seemed a shame that our comparatively ugly ships should desecrate such a fairy sea as this, but up we went nevertheless, to search out the upper reaches. Nothing of any suspicious nature was observed so we retired outside, where we parted company, the "Majestic" proceeding to Mudros, where we arrived late in the evening.

The next morning (Good Friday) we anchored a fair way up the harbour and proceeded to get off the two 6-inch howitzers, which we had shipped at Malta, but of which we had made scarcely any use. But what had been happening on the island? The place was crowded with troops. From the bridge we could see line upon line of tents, and troops moving everywhere on shore. It looked as though some big event was in the wind.

The weather was truly glorious, a moderately warm sun heightening the colours and the clear blue of the sky reflected in the smooth surface of the sea. In the evening we bathed in water that was like champagne, and clear as crystal. The following day we were given permission to land on the island. What a sight! It was like a gigantic fair. Streams of horses and mules were being landed from French troopships, while lighters discharged loads of hay and oats for feeding the beasts. On the landing-stage, which had been built out from the beach on rafts, to allow lighters and steamships to come alongside, there were huge piles of forage and gear, in great square heaps about twenty feet high.

Higher up the dust-heap that went by the name of " Road " and came over the tops of one's boots, there was a weird and wonderful collection of wooden shanties where one could purchase anything from a bottle of Black and White—which cost ten shillings—to a rotten egg or putrid fish which made known its existence a mile off.

AFTER THE BOMBARDMENT

The island native population had multiplied itself many times. Every imaginable tongue of the Near East was represented, and all human riff-raff that could make Lemnos seemed to have done so. Doubtless a fair proportion of the unsavoury throng were spies in the pay of the enemy—in fact, two had already been arrested. In the ramshackle bit of a village on the crest of the hill every house was a "drinking-house," and the atmosphere and life that abounded there were vile beyond words.

At the back of the village the Australians and New Zealanders had pitched their camp. On seeing that we possessed a football, they immediately pounced upon us, and we fixed up a game of "soccer," which ended in our favour.

In other parts of the island, under canvas, were Frenchmen, Indians, Zouaves, dark-skinned Senegalese, and various types of colonial infantry from every corner of the British Empire. Never was such an assortment of nationalities gathered together on one small island. With the dust and the mules and donkeys, and the jabber of strange tongues, and the mass of colours moving in the rich sunlight, and the ships of all classes and types resting placidly on the blue waters, the scene was one beyond all imagination. Envisage 30,000 men clad in a score of different ways, with their baggage and transport and animals—scores and scores of ships from picket-boat to Dreadnought, from collier to troopship—all packed within a few square miles of land and water! Invest all these with movement and colour, and what a human symphony one gets.

At 6 p.m. we wended our way to the pier, armed with some cheese and eggs, and still dizzy with the sights we had seen. Just before we left the pier General D'Amade's gear arrived. We heard that he was in charge of the French troops, and also, which was more important, that we were staying in the harbour for the night.

On the morrow we left for the Dardanelles, and commenced patrolling again. For three days we were employed at this exceedingly dull job, and in perfectly vile weather we proceeded up coast early in the morning of April, and met "Swiftsure" and "Ark Royal" with one destroyer and some minesweepers, the whole of us proceeding to Enos which lay about ten miles off. Two seaplanes went up from the "Ark Royal," but one of

AFTER THE BOMBARDMENT 111

them had a little engine trouble and fell into the sea. The pilot and observer were both rescued by our cutter.

Two mine-sweepers were sent ashore, along with a couple of steamboats with whalers in tow for the purpose of doing a bit of sounding, or else to draw the enemy's fire. If the latter had been the object, it was certainly successful, for when the boats were within three miles of the shore, the Turks opened fire on them, and compelled them to return. We scattered with shrapnel a group of Turks that were collecting on the beach, and then, the seaplane having returned and made its report, off we went, back to Tenedos.

For the next few days things continued to remain quiet, but the signs and portents of events pending increased every hour. Commander Samson arrived with machines, aviators, observers, and miscellaneous gear, all of which was established on land in quick time. Everywhere activity prevailed. The weather was getting warmer each day, and at nights it was very "stuffy" and gloomy, with all the deadlights down and no glimmer anywhere. The only relief to the blackness was the powerful searchlights from Chanak which flashed down the Straits in anticipation of a night-attack.

On the 14th an airman located a new battery up the Gulf of Saros, and off we went to deal with it. The airman accompanied us, so as to observe the shooting. Before long we had it to pieces, and were about to leave when the " Goeben," which was lying somewhere up in the Narrows, opened fire on us at 13,000 yards. In order to show that the Gur-Turk-Hun is by no means a bad shot, I give the correct result of the shots as taken by myself. First, second, and 3rd shots, 300, 400, and 300 yards over. Fourth shot (2 rounds) 400 yards short. Fifth, sixth, and seventh shots, 200 to 400 yards short. A lot of the pieces of shell fell on board ; the quarter deck in particular was strewn with them. At 13,000 yards this is not at all bad.

We continued patrolling for the next few days. While the Turks in the peninsula were feverishly strengthening their positions. They did it all at night, and each day we could see the results of their prodigious labours. On the hills and slopes leading from the great Achi Baba we could see rows and rows of trenches, miles long, and, as far as we could make out, very broad and substantial.

AFTER THE BOMBARDMENT 113

It would be a bad place to land an army, for, in addition to the fortifications, the natural configuration of the land was all to the advantage of the defenders. It was one confused mass of little hills and valleys, running right down to the shore. When we stood in-shore we could see a network of barbed wire running in every direction. We got the guns on to a section of it, but the result was disappointing. It would be ghastly fighting in such circumstances. On the 17th we heard that the submarine E15 had run ashore up the Dardanelles near Kephez Point, and that the crew had been made prisoners. The next day we decided to attempt to blow her up, as the Turks were trying to salve her. The " Triumph " and ourselves were honoured by being the ships chosen to carry out this operation. Every precaution was taken, for we should have to penetrate the Straits to some considerable distance, and there was no knowing what Abdul might have in store for us. The " Triumph " led the way and the " Majestic " followed close behind. They started firing at us almost immediately, and, apprehending our purpose, obscured the submarine from view by means of smoke-balls. The exceedingly strong defences did not permit our getting nearer than 12,000 yards or so, and to have carried out a bombardment at that distance with the target hidden from view would have been only wasting good powder and shot. We were under heavy shell-fire all the time, but not one of them struck the ship. We retired from the Straits and awaited further orders.

We hadn't to wait very long ; the submarine must never be allowed to get into the Turks' hands in a serviceable condition. It was resolved to attempt a night-attack and two picket boats were to be employed— one from the " Triumph " and one from the " Majestic." If ever there was a death or glory mission this was it. Volunteers were called for, and instantly far more men than were required stepped forward.

After all, there is something glorious about men despite their little shortcomings. Here was a task so difficult and dangerous, that only volunteers were accepted, and to see them all step forward as one man did one's heart good. There could have been no doubt as to the risk it entailed. Those two boats were to go right up into the jaws of death, through a narrow channel lined with guns, and with the searchlights, seeking, seeking relentlessly. One small shell in close proximity, and a boat would be gone like a stone —a rifle could have drilled a hole through such frail craft—and yet the men were simply dying to be in the " beano " !

The crews chosen, the two boats started under the cover of an inky black night, each with torpedo-dropping gear, to which was attached a 14-inch torpedo. Using the screen of the Gallipoli cliffs, they began to creep up to the point from which they would make their final dash to Kephez Point. A spark from a funnel, the flicker of a light, even the noisy thud of a carelessly controlled engine would have been sufficient to bring them under the glare of the searchlight, and at the mercy of the guns. At the wheel under the cover of the small armed shield of steel, was the coxswain, peering into the compass, dimly lighted by one candle. In his keeping were the lives of the whole crew. The merest deviation from the charted course would spell ruin for the expedition and disaster to the men. But he was a man of iron, and of great experience; the hand on the wheel never wavered, and the boats crept on through the blackness, nearer, ever nearer the point from which the final dash would be made.

At last! The boats veered a little and struck straight for the bend at the approach of the Narrows. Nothing had gone wrong with the manipulation of the boat; it was just sheer bad luck—out of the darkness two great streaks of light came, and landed full on the two boats. Instantly hell was let loose. From all sides came a fusillade of gun and rifle fire. Blinded and bewildered for a moment, the boats endeavoured to escape from the glare; but there was no escape, so the boats simply went straight on, the coxswains, with almost superhuman faculty, still reading their compasses correctly. Shot and shell were rained upon them, but still they drove on, dodging the fire in an inexplicable way. But where was the E 15? In that brilliant glare the darkness beyond was intensified a hundred-fold, and the Turks were careful to keep their rays off our quarry. Just when it seemed that all hopes of finding the submarine were gone, a wonderful stroke of luck favoured us. The outer edge of one of the searchlights played for an instant a little wide, and there, outlined against the black cliff behind, was the E 15. A few seconds later the "Majestic" picket-boat fired her torpedo. What happened after that it is difficult to say. There was a deep roar and a terrific flash as the torpedo exploded, and then almost simultaneously a shell burst in the stern-sheets, wrecking it and mortally wounding one of the crew. The boat began to sink fast, but, just as it was nearly submerged, the " Triumph's " boat fired its torpedo and came rushing along to rescue the crew. The thing was timed to a nicety, and as the boat sank the last man was taken from her. Then off went the plucky little picket-boat down stream with her double crew, deluged with lead and shrapnel the whole way.

How they reached the ship is a mystery, but they did so without any further casualties of any kind. The wounded man died on the journey and was buried next day with full naval honours. In the morning we learned that the torpedoes had found their mark and that little was left of the E 15 except scrap-iron.

The next day we did patrol work, and then on April 20th proceeded to Mudros, where we witnessed a magnificent spectacle. As far as the eye could see was nothing but ships, ships, ships—warships, transports, hospital-ships, store-ships, balloon-ships, ammunition-ships, refilling-ships, colliers, frozen-meat ships, water-tank carriers, mine-sweepers, tugs—every kind of ship one could possibly imagine.

When I saw the Canadians arrive I considered it a fine sight, but it was simply nothing compared with this vast assembly. A day or two later I made up my mind to count them, but I only got to two hundred, and then gave it up as a hopeless job.

We coaled ship and took in ammunition, and then waited for the mighty attack that was going to be launched against the Turks.

We learned that we were going to form part of the covering ships for the landing of the Australians and New Zealanders at Gaba Tepe. Most of us were surprised that the landing would take place on the Gallipoli Peninsula; we imagined it would have been effected farther up on the mainland. There could be no doubt that the Turks would be quite prepared for us wherever we landed down there, seeing that it was so close to our own base.

We had a few boat practices for landing troops, and a lecture on the operation in general, and then waited for the Great Event.

Later in the day troopships began to pass

AFTER THE BOMBARDMENT 119

outside, crowded with troops, and bands playing. There was plenty of cheering on board them, but nobody on the "Majestic" cheered. Why I do not know. It has always been a mystery to me—unless it was because they had a very good idea of the task that awaited those troops.

Up to a late hour the ships passed out all crowded from end to end. A sight of interest was a steamer called the "River Clyde" which had large holes cut in her side. The idea was to run her ashore, so as to form a kind of landing-stage, the holes permitting a number of men to get ashore in quick time—she was carrying about 2,000 troops.

The next day (April 24th) we began to make a move. At 2 p.m. we proceeded outside to pick up the remainder of our squadron—Rear-Admiral C. F. Thursby, C.M.G., being in command of the Gaba Tepe expedition. The squadron consisted of the following ships. Battleships: "Queen," "London," "Prince of Wales," "Triumph," "Majestic." Cruiser: "Bacchante." Destroyers: "Beagle," "Bulldog," "Foxhound," "Scourge," "Colne," "Usk," "Chelmer," "Ribble." Seaplane-carrier:

"Ark Royal." Balloon-ship "Monica," and about twenty trawlers and various lighters, —the troopships following behind.

The first landing-party was carried on board the "Queen," "London," and "Prince of Wales." The "Triumph" and "Majestic" supplied boat crews for landing.

We shaped our course for Gaba Tepe at a slow pace, as we did not want to get there too early, since we could do nothing until the moon had set. At 4 a.m. he sunk below the horizon and the moment of our great venture had come.

CHAPTER X

THE GREAT LANDING

IT was very dark now, and we got the boats ready to take up their stations alongside the troopships. Everything was beautifully prepared—not a thing left to chance. Oars were muffled, and what speech was necessary was made in low whispers. To have shown the merest glimmer of light would have ruined the whole thing.

We shoved off from the "Majestic," took up our position near the troopship, and were soon filled with troops. Everything seemed very weird and ghostly. Men made signs and motions to each other, but this method of communication failed in the main, for the darkness enwrapped everything.

The beach we could not see, but we shoved the boat along in the direction in which we knew it lay. I shall never forget that trip —it seemed endless. There was no sound but the very faint splash of the water on the muffled oars, and the boats moved along in the gloom for all the world like the cargoes which old Charon was mythically supposed to transport over the Styx.

After what seemed to be an interminable period the suspense was broken by the report of a rifle and the light of a flare on shore. That was the beginning of things. Very soon a Maxim was blazing away at us, hitting a good many men in our boat. It was still dark, and we could gain no idea as to how things were going, but we determined to land—the Colonials were mad to get at grips with Abdul, and only death would have prevented a man from getting there.

The first grey of the morning was coming, dispersing the gloom and revealing the beach not far ahead. But with the departure of darkness came the terrors of the day. Shrapnel shell came shrieking at us from the shore. One dropped right into the centre of our boat and wrought tremendous havoc. It would have been suicide to have stayed there longer, so overboard we went and made for the nearest cover. Very few of us got there, for the sea was torn by the flying shrapnel bullets, and many a poor fellow

THE GREAT LANDING

found a watery grave. The other boats were having a similar experience; some of the crews took to the water, but others were beached successfully.

Once on shore we closed in to the right a bit, where there was a little more shelter and things were not so hot. All round us were the hills running up in precipitous slopes. A great cheer went up from our right, and the order came to charge the hill. Off we went in a mad rush. There was no holding the troops now, for they had smelt blood and powder, and many of them had seen their comrades drop helplessly beside them. Most of them tore off all their equipment, leaving them with only the rifle and bayonet and ammunition stuffed in their pockets.

Up that awful hill they went "hanging on by their eyelashes." Shrapnel and shot of every description were rained on them, but still they went forward, cursing and singing and mad with the rage of battle.

As it grew lighter the ships opened fire over the top of the hills with a view to keeping the enemy in check. A steady stream of troops were landing now from the various ships, and soon there was a good number of men on the beach to carry on the fight.

The conflict went on hour after hour, both sides fighting with dogged tenacity. Inch by inch the hill was gained, bloody sweat dripping from the eager fighting men. They were mad with the thought of the many who had died and were wounded in the boats without the opportunity of getting in a blow.

From the top of the hill we could see two of the boats that had suffered so badly and had lost practically all their party in the first attempt. The wounded men were being sent straight off to the ships in case of a retirement; but we didn't have to retire. It would have broken the men's hearts to have retired just then.

The Turks were keeping up a terrific fire all over the beach, but still the work went on, and men were landed and others taken away to the ships.

By some mistake we had landed the men about one mile to the left of Gaba Tepe, but it turned out to be a blessing in disguise, for the men were able to get close in under the hills, digging themselves in, and thus securing themselves to a certain extent from the shrapnel and snipers' fire. Had they been landed at the place allotted God knows what

THE GREAT LANDING 125

would have happened, as there was no protection there whatsoever, the hills under which they now sheltered completely commanding the open beach at Gaba Tepe.

A lot of the shells which fell upon the beach failed to explode, which shortcoming saved the lives of hundreds. They were filled with all kinds of rubbish. I saw a brass door-dangle in one, whilst others contained pieces of china. Some even contained dust-road sweepings. It looked as though some one had played a dirty trick on Abdul.

In the afternoon the Turks made a great counter-attack, launching thousands of troops at us, but defeat was staved off with the help of the ships, which poured salvos of shrapnel into them.

Away along the beach to the left was a boat full of wounded or dead men. Desperate attempts were made to recover them, but the Turks had a machine-gun trained on the spot, and as it was right in the open the attempts had to be abandoned. In any case, it was doubtful if any of the poor chaps were still alive.

The hospital ships had all left crowded with the wounded, so the battleships and troopships had to be utilised for this purpose.

The "Majestic" had ninety-six wounded on board, all cheerful and full of fun. The only sorrow that they had was having to leave the fight so early. No praise could be too great for these sons of the Motherland. The way they went into action was staggering. They laughed at obstacles, and never knew the fear of death. It might have been a gigantic football match for all they cared. Physically they were magnificent, at times literally performing gymnastic feats, scaling almost perpendicular heights by sheer strength of muscle and agility of limb. God help the Turk when once they got hand to hand!

The first line of trenches were taken at the point of the bayonet, and the men were busy consolidating the position. Of our party that landed only one man was wounded, which confirmed my conviction that the old "Majestic" carried luck with her.

After dark the ships crept closer in and played their searchlights on the extreme flanks, so as to observe any reinforcements from either side.

After a cold and uneventful night, the day broke fine, and found the troops still clinging to the high ledges that had been so hardly won. The landing-place had been shifted a little

THE GREAT LANDING

to the right, to be nearer the shelter which the hill provided. The boat journeys, however, to and from the beach were fraught with danger, for they had to pass through a zone of fire constantly menaced by the Turkish guns. Many of the boats were hit passing through the bullet-swept area.

Every hour more troops and guns, ammunition, donkeys, and mules were landing, and the beach began to reproduce the scene I witnessed at Mudros. Gear and fodder and food were piled up everywhere, turning the outlandish place into a kind of seaside holiday resort. Even the dugouts began to boast curtains, and roads were already beginning to appear on the sides of the hills. Away to the right the troops had advanced about 800 yards and a field-battery of howitzers had been mounted in a good position, from which they were able to blaze away at Turks hidden behind a ridge where the ships' guns could not penetrate.

About noon a fort on ships somewhere up the Narrows began to open fire at us. Some of the shells came unpleasantly near, and several ships had to make a move. All the wounded from the "Majestic" were transferred to a hospital ship which steamed away in fine spirits, the men giving three cheers for the " Majestic " as they went off.

On shore we were still holding our own, making a bit of an advance in the evening. Abdul did not like the bayonet at all, squealing with fright when it came to that. The Colonials simply loved this kind of work. Nothing delighted them more than to know that the bayonet was coming into operation. For sheer devilry and love of close fighting commend me to these boys from " down under."

The country around was terrible for fighting in. You could hardly move for the interwoven mass of small trees and shrubs that grow unchecked on every side. A good many casualties occurred the day before through this same disadvantageous feature of the country. As the troops advanced some would push too far inland, and lose contact with the main body through the maze of undergrowth which prevented their seeing more than a few yards in any direction. Then they would have to fight their way back again, exposed to the fire of every lurking Turkish sniper.

I found that the boat which had brought me from the ship had suffered worse than I

THE GREAT LANDING

had imagined. Out of the party of fifty-four, apparently only two of us reached the beach alive. The others were doubtless cut to pieces with shrapnel, and it was obviously impossible for a wounded man to make land.

The battery that had been doing such frightful work on the beach had been silenced by the ships, and in the afternoon the latter closed inshore and commenced a terrific bombardment of the Turkish positions; such a din it would be impossible to beat—everything banging off at once and shells of every size and description, from both sides, falling all over the place. The ships' fire caused terrible destruction among the Turks. At times they were fairly blown out of their trenches.

The worst thing we had to contend with was the snipers, who would disguise themselves in all manner of ways, colouring their faces and dressing up to represent trees, shrubs, and what not. They would hide in small holes with just a stone to cover up the entrance, making it almost impossible to locate them.

The few prisoners which we brought in, with trembling limbs, vouched for the effectiveness of our bombardment, describing it, in quavering voices, as "infernal."

The weather had turned gloriously, and not a ripple disturbed the blue limpidness of the water. The strangest thing of all was to see the troops bathing on the beach with shrapnel bursting all round them. They had become acclimatised to the conditions by now, and treated Abdul's "birthday presents" with the utmost contempt.

There was no spell at all, night and day it was just the same. When you came out of the trenches you would immediately turn and make roads, or carry water or munitions to the top of the hill. Yet the good spirits and fun never waned for a minute; on every hand you would hear tales and jokes and laughter. All through the night the Turks kept up a heavy fire with their rifles and machine-guns. I suppose they were in a mortal funk of a night-attack, and wanted to show us they were still there.

At 5 a.m. the next day (April 27th) I saw the ships begin to "in nets" and "up anchor" preparatory to commencing their day's work. The boat that was stranded along the beach under the Turkish fire had been recovered, but all the men that were

THE GREAT LANDING 131

in her were dead, and were buried at night. The Turks continued to send down shells from the Narrows, but scarcely any damage resulted, which was miraculous considering that there was something like two hundred ships of all classes there.

The balloon was doing excellent work "spotting," as also were seaplanes that went up from the "Monica."

We were still hanging on to our positions, having advanced a little to the north. The Fisherman's Hut was smashed up with a few well-directed shells, and a party of men went scouting around it; but, as they were sniped at from every quarter, they were forced to retire to their advanced post. One of the places on shore had been christened "Hell Spit," and a most appropriate name it was, too, for death was always present in that bullet-swept quarter.

The next morning I was ready to drop from fatigue, having had scarcely any sleep since I first landed. By a stroke of luck I managed to get back to the ship, which was a pleasant relief from the terrors and hardships of the land campaign. But I was glad to have been in the thick of it for those few days, for it opened my eyes to many things and most of all filled me with admiration for the boys from " down under," who fought with unimaginable coolness and bravery in the most trying and adverse circumstances.

The ship was now looking after the left flank of the army and incidentally giving the Turks a warm time. We got in some very good practice during the day, some of our shells pitching right into the Turkish trenches. There was no doubt as to the havoc it caused, for we could see fragments of Turks being blown over the sky-line. One poor devil was blown up, whole, about sixty yards into the air, spinning round like a cart-wheel the whole time.

We were subjected to the usual bombardment of Jack Johnsons and what not, but with our usual luck escaped. One huge shell pitched about twenty yards from us and smothered the ship with spray, but caused no damage. This kind of shell made a terrific noise when it exploded, and turned the water black for a distance of about fifty yards all round. Bits of the shell would fly all over the place, many on the ship itself.

Another danger we had to beware of on the ship was the sniper on shore, who delighted to have pot shots at us when we were standing close in. No end of rifle-bullets were found on the forecastle and quarter-deck.

I sometimes think that our "luck" was more due to human agency than to the gods. Our Captain—H. F. G. Talbot—handled the ship with the most consummate skill and coolness. Among the ship's company he was known as "shot dodger," on account of his manœuvring the ship among the falling shells, and hardly ever getting struck in a vital place. I have watched him do this with the shells screaming overhead, and have been amazed at the way in which he eluded them. At the worst times he would order every man—including officers—under cover, but he himself would stand all alone on the fore shelter deck giving his orders in the calmest possible voice, as though he were utterly unconscious of any danger.

No wonder the crew worshipped him! It is this practice of "example" which brings out the best qualities in men, and spurs them on to the noblest actions.

For the next few days we continued to protect the left flank. On shore the fight was going on without halt. To the left the troops were making progress, but it was slow, for difficulties were enormous. The second ridge of hills behind the landing was fully 600 feet high, and would prove a fearful thing to tackle. Looking from the sea on to the hills already taken, it seemed impossible that such a feat could have been achieved. Every foot of the precipitous slope had been scaled under a murderous fire. Any one seeing the height in the light of day would have deemed the task impossible, and yet these magnificent chaps had given the lie to that assertion, and were clinging on to the ground so hardly won, with the full determination to hold it, whatever happened. Verily my admiration grew more intense each time I looked at it. I believe they would have taken hell itself, if they had been so instructed.

We were doing great execution ashore by all appearances, for constantly we got the signal " O.K.," which meant that we were placing the shells where they were wanted. The targets in most cases were out of our line of vision and our sights were laid and adjusted by the results of the " spotting " on shore. We continued the work all through the night.

THE GREAT LANDING

The first of May, true to tradition, broke gloriously fine. It was certainly the strangest May 1st I had ever spent, and I doubt not that every man would have said the same. It was difficult to realise the true situation with the sun enhancing all the beautiful natural colourings and the sea lapping gently on the beach. The domestic part of the work went on peacefully. Men bathed, washed their clothes, and dried them in the sunlight, whistling or singing the while. The ships rained their daily messengers of death into the Turkish trenches; the troops on shore fought and sweated throughout the long day. A lucky shell from the Narrows would drop on a collier and kill one or two men—but the struggle would go on without let or hindrance. One day was very much like another, and one soon began to reconcile it as part of one's "job."

A lot of the Turkish shells were still failing to explode, and many were collected from the beach and found to contain rubbish.

Work never ceased. It was one continuously animated picture. Boats were going to and from the shore, laden with all kinds of cargo from French troops to mule fodder. On the beach the mountain of provisions and ammunition was bigger than ever. A stream of mules wended its way in the sunlight up to the gunners on the hill-top, laden with shells and other things. On the fringe of the sea naked figures splashed about in the water, and in every direction was movement and action, colour, and the sound of bitter strife—a pleasant enough picture to gaze upon, but not to think about.

Early in the morning of May 3rd a small party landed at Niebruncia Bay, a point running out a little north of Gaba Tepe, and surprised a party of Turks who were manning an observation station and directing their guns on to our troops. There was a sharp little fight, but the Turks were soon overcome, and the party returned, after destroying the telephone, etc., with twenty prisoners. Our casualties were slight—two men wounded.

For the remainder of the day things were very quiet on the sea, all the "Jack Johnsons" being good enough to miss us.

On the following night all the ships opened up a terrific bombardment on the high ridge, and kept it up for thirty minutes. It was too dark to see what results were attained,

THE GREAT LANDING 137

but it must have been hell for any Turkish troops that were up there.

In the morning a landing-party tried to get a footing on Gaba Tepe Point. They came off the destroyers in ships' boats, succeeded in landing, and were going up the side of the cliff, when they came upon an impassable mass of barbed wire, and simultaneously the Turks opened fire from the front of the hill with rifles and machine-guns, and from the left with shrapnel.

The party, caught between the two fires, was in a critical position. The boats had left for the ships in order to bring a further landing-party, and the poor fellows were left stranded. Fortunately it didn't take the ships long to realise the situation. All the small craft that had a gun aboard and all the destroyers rushed to the Point and opened up a raking fire inland. The larger ships supplemented this with heavy fire from a distance.

In the meantime steamboats with ship's boats—each containing two men—in tow, made for the beach. The boats were dropped and the two men in each boat got them near enough to the shore for the party to re-embark. The party, scattered about under what small cover they had succeeded in finding, then rushed for all they were worth down to the boats.

There was a hail of lead from Abdul, and some of the men fell, but they were all picked up and got safely into the boats. The steamboats had already turned about and were waiting for the boats to clear the beach so that they might take them in tow again. A few minutes, and all was safely accomplished, and the rescued party well on its way to the ships.

All was done in an incredibly short time, and the men responsible for it deserve the highest praise. By their quickness and skill they literally tore from the jaws of death a considerable party of men, who in a very short time would have been completely annihilated.

CHAPTER XI

BACK TO THE DARDANELLES

ON Tuesday, May 6th, we bade good-bye to Gaba Tepe and all the brave boys that we had been proud to work with. I had no doubt they would miss old " Twin Funnels "—as they called us, owing to our funnels being abreast—and personally I was very sorry to leave them, much as I hated Gaba Tepe with all its bloodshed and horror.

The memory of that place will always live in my brain, and the brave deeds that took place there would fill many volumes. So numerous were they, indeed, as to make a faithful record impossible.

We left Gaba Tepe to relieve the " Prince George," down at the Dardanelles—she had been badly knocked about and holed below the water-line.

Arrived at the Dardanelles we soon got to work and established communication with the signal-station, who seemed very glad to hear of our arrival. Our job was to look after the right flank of the French troops who were carrying on operations on land.

In a very short time we opened fire on the Turkish trenches, which were quite close to Morto Bay, where the French were landing a lot of troops preparatory to a night attack. We got quite a lively reception, the Turks opening fire on us from both sides of the Straits; but their shooting was extraordinarily bad, and we didn't receive a scratch.

What a change at Seddul Bahr from when I last saw it! Then it was a deserted, desolate place; now it looked as though some great town had sprung out of the earth. The whole place was buzzing with action and excitement. Out at sea was a regular fleet of vessels—small tugs, merchant ships, colliers, rushing all over the place. Men were going ashore to take their place in the firing-line, and others were coming from the furnace to be patched up by the doctors, that they might, perchance, fight again.

The "River Clyde" was there, but we heard she had not proved very successful in her new vocation. Many men were killed

BACK TO THE DARDANELLES 141

before they could land—in fact, it appeared that the landing in general was a very bloody and costly affair. All things considered, it was a wonder that any one was landed at all. But here they were, and they seemed to have established themselves very firmly.

The Turkish prisoners were busy making roads along the beach under the old forts, and also running a kind of pier to the " River Clyde."

At 8 p.m. we went outside to anchor for the night, but we were at it again by 3 o'clock the next morning. After the nets were taken in, we proceeded up the Straits to look after the French. We could see the effect of the previous night's advance. Slowly the French were gaining ground, the " Majestic " steaming abreast of them. At 7 a.m. there was a heavy counter-attack by the Turks, but the French held their ground stubbornly, and then immediately counter-charged, driving the Turks right over the cliffs. We then opened fire on them at short range—2,000 yards—and the carnage was sickening. They were lying on the cliffs in hundreds—I doubt if many escaped. The signal-station reported that our fire was doing tremendous execution, and that the French general was very pleased. We kept up a very heavy fire until 1 p.m., and then got relieved by the "Canopus" and went outside to anchor. We had a quiet afternoon, and I watched the advance from the fore-top. I saw some magnificent rushes all along the line, but the distance was too great to follow the battle in detail. It must have been terrible work out there, for the Turk had the advantage of knowing the country and was naturally well sheltered in prepared positions.

At 8 p.m. we got under way again, and went into the Straits for night work. This was a very quiet sort of business, for the Turk was not much of a night-bird. He would keep up his infernal popping the whole night through, but he hadn't a taste for venturing abroad. Had he done so, he would have had plenty of chances. Just fancy a battleship in enemy waters, patrolling without lights and under strict instructions not to fire a gun unless ordered to do so. What use we were up there, Heaven only knows! It was a mercy the Turks didn't send down a torpedo-boat, or something, at us.

Anyhow, we weren't leaving much to chance on the old "Magic-Stick," and kept a good look-out the whole time. As for a sleep, such a thing was not dreamed of—that was a thing of the past. We hadn't known what a proper night's rest was since the memorable April 25th.

The night dragged on its weary way, and all one craved for was the morning, so that one might be able to work and forget some of the worst features.

At 5 a.m. the signal-station requested us to open fire on the trenches again, which we did with great pleasure. The Turkish dead were still lying thick on the side of the cliff above Eski Hissarlik Point—I counted over 300 of them from the ship. The French had been down to take away and bury their dead, but fortunately they were comparatively few.

We were still troubled with shells from the Asiatic side, but managed to escape them by some means or other. It seemed mysterious that we should be so fortunate. Most of the other ships had been hit several times, and yet here we were gaily steaming along.

When a shot did hit us, it was invariably negligible—something seemed to go wrong with it as soon as it discovered it had landed on the "Majestic." That afternoon a shell came through the after shelter-deck, smashed one of the ladders that led up to it, went through the bulk-head into the navigator's cabin, thence through the deck, where it lodged, by reason of the copper-driving band, right over the petty officer's mess, which was full at the time. Why it didn't explode, Heaven only knows, but it didn't, and the crowd in there have a lot to be thankful for.

A young marine picked up the live shell in a whirl of excitement and rushed to the fore bridge with it, to show the captain. Everybody crowded round to get a glimpse of the relic, and a murmur of intense disappointment went up when the captain ordered it to be thrown overboard.

On the 9th we were still protecting the French right flank. Things seemed to be a bit quieter in-shore. The French were well established in their new ground, which they had won, and were busily engaged in strengthening their position. All the time fresh troops were landing from the troopships and pressing up into the line. The Turks were a little luckier in their shooting that morning. We narrowly missed catching a big one. The "Agamemnon" was badly hit, her funnel and ventilators being torn to ribbons. The "Cornwallis" also got hit, but there was not

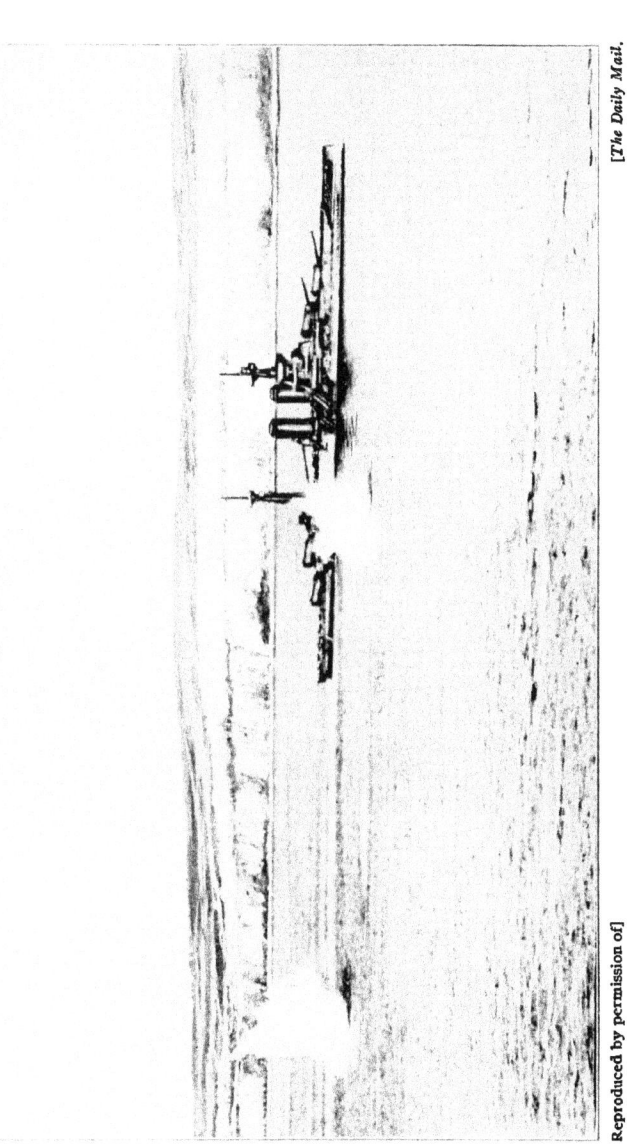

Reproduced by permission of] [*The Daily Mail.*
ONE OF OUR BATTLESHIPS FIRED AT FROM TURKISH FORTS IN THE STRAITS.

BACK TO THE DARDANELLES 145

a considerable amount of damage done, and very few casualties.

For two hours we saturated the Turkish trenches with shrapnel, as the French wanted to attempt a fresh advance. After the bombardment they started off, and we watched the sight with enthralling interest. They went straight for the Turkish trenches like a terrier at a rat, and cleared out the occupants in quick time. The Turks broke in every direction, and then came the French cavalry, who had been waiting, carefully concealed behind some broken walls, to the left of the infantry. It was a magnificent sight. They charged right through the flying Turks, the sun flashing on the blades of their swords as they slashed right and left. They had the game entirely in their own hands, and we were like spectators at a football match, watching them and cheering with joy.

A lot of prisoners were taken, and marched across the shell-scarred battle-field behind. But still the hail of lead continued, for Abdul seemed to have an endless supply.

At 1 p.m. we were relieved by the "Albion" and proceeded outside to anchor, etc.—the etcetera covers a host of duties: coaling ship, taking in ammunition, and various other items connected with the working of the ship which was done when "off duty." We anchored a little farther up the coast than usual—above Cape Hellas, where we could see well in over the land. The colouring was gorgeous—blues and reds and sepias intermingled with the soft tints everywhere the eye roamed. The more brilliant colours were fruit blossoms, but it seemed doubtful if ever the fruit which grew from them would ever be gathered in that valley of death. All around was the turmoil of battle—a continuous rattle of musketry and roar of big guns. Even the heavens failed to escape, for high up in the blue, small white clouds were appearing as if by magic, and one saw that they were shell bursts and that an aeroplane was being sträfed.

Most discomforting of all was the news that a submarine was on its way from Germany to add variety to the conflict and to carry war into the three elements. It wasn't nice to contemplate the arrival of this new visitor with a huge fleet like ours for a target.

On shore a large party of Greeks and Engineers were making a fine new road well in under the protection of the cliffs, for the

BACK TO THE DARDANELLES 147

Turks had been unusually energetic of late in throwing a lot of "big stuff" into the camp. Only that afternoon we saw a party of men and horses blown to atoms just over the edge of the cliff, and another party on the beach suffered badly. We saw the remains of the latter party collected together for burial. Such sights are ghastly, but one simply *has* to get used to them. The large shells make a terrific disturbance, throwing a cloud of sand fully 200 feet into the air.

Just before anchoring for the night we heard that the Gurkhas were going to operate after dark, and wondered what Abdul would think of the dusky little warrior and his nocturnal ways.

At 3 o'clock next morning we were at it again. There was no rest or respite of any kind. The few hours of subconsciousness which we called sleep were not sufficient to constitute "a break." The strain was beginning to tell on the ship's company, and, to make things worse, rations ran low, and we had but ½ lb. of bread per day, supplemented with ship's biscuits and occasional fresh meat.

Nobody grumbled, because they all realised the vast difficulties in provisioning a great gathering of men like this, in foreign waters, where every pound of food had to be carried thousands of miles. We were the oldest ship up there, and were handicapped a lot by having no bakery aboard, nor any facilities for keeping fresh meat. It was a marvel to me that we got bread at all under the circumstances, and it reflected great credit upon the poor cooks with only one galley to do all the work.

At times the " sponge " for the bread was spoiled by the heavy gun-fire, and then we lived on biscuits entirely!

For the next few days we continued looking after the French flank. Then the news spread abroad that enemy submarines were in the vicinity, and one by one the newer ships began to make the base for safety. Soon it looked as though only the old "crocks" remained. It was rather disquieting, but we didn't mind much.

Things began to get much quieter at Seddul Bahr. Occasionally we dropped a few shells there, but nothing of any consequence happened.

The French at Seddul Bahr were suffering a lot from big shells whose origin they were unable to locate. We had an idea they came from caves on the side of Achi Baba, but as soon as an aeroplane went up to spot the firing ceased, and so we were compelled to accept these daily visitors as a kind of natural manifestation.

CHAPTER XII

LOSS OF H.M.S. "GOLIATH"

I HAD just dropped off to sleep (May 13th) when I was awakened by the voice of Boatswain's mate calling away all boats. There was something unusual in this procedure, so I was out of my hammock and up on deck in quick time. There I learned that the "Goliath," which lay ahead of us, had either been torpedoed or blown up.

At the captain's request I called away all life-boats, manned them with crews, and got them off. It was an inky-black night, so I rushed up to the fore bridge and got the searchlights ready for action, which was soon done, as they were fitted with automatic gear for signalling purposes. I had grave doubts about using the lights, as we had received orders that no lights were to be shown up there. I decided to risk it, and up went the lights—orders or no orders. What a

LOSS OF H.M.S. "GOLIATH"

sight met our eyes! The "Goliath" was gone, but in the water were struggling men and floating wreckage of every description.

The "Goliath" must have sunk in less than three minutes. Either she was struck with two torpedoes or there were two explosions aboard, for two distinct reports were heard from the "Majestic."

The current was running at four to five knots, sweeping the struggling mass of humanity down upon us. Many of the poor chaps had already succumbed, and were being kept afloat by the life-belts which they wore. The crews of the boats were working like mad to save every possible man, but it was little enough they could do. All our ship's company were ranged up along the ship's side with ropes and belts blown up ready to heave to any one who came near enough. Everything that would float was heaved overboard in the hope that lives might be saved thereby.

Some of the men that we succeeded in getting on board, told us that they thought we were steaming ahead right through them and had tried to keep clear of us—doubtless they never realised the strength of the current, and would naturally get that impression.

Farther out on our starboard about fifty men were clinging to some floating gear. We kept the light on them, hoping that a boat would see them and go to their rescue. Other boats from different ships were soon on the scene, but the loss of life must have been terrible, for the current would hamper the work of rescue.

A signalman in our mess, who was on watch at the time, told us it was a Turkish torpedo-boat that had fired the torpedo. The " Goliath " hailed the boat and got some sort of reply, but almost simultaneously the torpedo struck and all was over with the good old ship. Our boats saved in all sixty men, who were eventually taken on board the " Lord Nelson."

The tragedy greatly affected the ship's company, for the sight of those poor fellows struggling in the water, and the realisation of the swiftness of the catastrophe, were sufficient to unnerve the strongest men.

We received orders that no more battle-ships were to go up patrolling at night, so we remained at anchor outside, still thinking of the tragedy and wondering when our turn might come.

For the next few days we carried out the

LOSS OF H.M.S. "GOLIATH" 153

same old routine, protecting the French right and firing an occasional shot at suspicious objects. May 18th was my Navy birthday, and I didn't hesitate to wish myself " many happy returns of the day "—it seemed so very appropriate just then, with Turkish shells flying around and a submarine hunting for prey.

Later in the day the Turks were lucky enough to get a hit home, though I am glad to say that no casualties resulted. It broke up our signal-house on the after-bridge and also riddled one of our large after ventilators. The bridge was a complete wreck, the planking ripped to ribbons, and the stension and rails blown clean away. I took it as a birthday present for me, since I was in charge of that bridge.

However, there is another side to this incident which has a certain psychological interest. Just before the house was struck, I was inside mending some flags that had been torn, and a R.N.R. man was on watch on top of it, watching for aeroplanes. All the time shells were screaming through the air, and eventually, unable to stand the strain any longer, he came down to me and said he couldn't stay up there any longer.

I could see that he was in a very bad state of "nerves," and, taking into consideration that he was one of the survivors from the "Ocean," I suggested that we should go below and smoke a pipe together. It was obviously no use his "carrying on" in his present condition. He had gone ghastly white and was apparently bordering on the breaking point. We descended the ladder and had no sooner reached the bottom when "bang!" came the shell, and the room we had left but a few seconds was in ruins.

One hardly likes to draw any inference from such happenings, they are so consistently accepted as coincidence that to suggest other possibilities is only to court scepticism; yet I cannot help thinking that the general scheme of things and even such small details as this are in the hands of some governing power and that premonitions—conscious or sub-conscious—are given to us for an express purpose. In my own life they have been so numerous as to remove any doubts in my mind.

I could not help noticing the change in the ship's company due to the cumulative nerve strain. They sought cover with greater promptitude than at first. In the early days

LOSS OF H.M.S. "GOLIATH" 155

they were all keen to see what was going on, and curious as to the result of an enemy shot; but that had all vanished. Men are but human, after all, and when the first thrill and excitement have grown stale, circumstances are observed in their true perspective.

Most of the shells were being fired from the Asiatic side, and it was almost impossible to locate the battery that fired them, as they appeared to shift the position from time to time. Their favourite target was the village of Seddul Bahr, into which they pumped all kinds of shell of large calibre, causing considerable damage and uneasiness.

We could always tell when that particular battery was firing, as there was a peculiar screech to the shell as it passed over us, a nasty kind of sound that never failed to send a little shiver down one's back.

My birthday passed away in similar fashion to a score of other days, but I couldn't help wondering whether it was ordained that I should see another birthday and in what circumstances.

The next day (May 19th) was the twenty-fifth day of continuous bombardment, and was likely to be far from the last. How long could the human mind endure the nerve-shattering trial? I was dismayed to realise how "jumpy" I was getting. The narrow escape of the previous day had told on me more than I expected. Sleep! how I yearned for sleep; but there was no sleep in that torment. Some of the men never even attempted to get their hammocks, but remained on deck sitting about all night. The end must come soon—flesh and blood could not endure it indefinitely.

For the signalmen there was no escape; whatever happened they must stick to their work, for they were "the eyes of the Fleet," upon whom safety largely depended. Most of all I pitied the men from the "Ocean"; theirs was indeed a hard lot. How glad we were when the time came to anchor outside! —but even then there was no peace for us, for we knew that enemy submarines were about, and to rest with that menace hanging over us was impossible.

At 8 o'clock the next morning up we went again as a bombarding ship, for the Asiatic side, but soon after the "Cornwallis" relieved us and took over the French right flank. She opened fire on the Asiatic side, and got an exceedingly hot reply from Abdul, which compelled her to drop astern. They then turned their guns on to us, but we got off comparatively lightly, with only a few hits aft, and no casualties. We could not retaliate, as we hadn't the slightest idea of the position of the battery. Later on an airman went up to spot for us, and we were delighted to think that we should have a chance to hit back. We soon got the range from the airman, and opened fire, but Abdul was getting wise at the game, and was cute enough to hold his fire, so we had to take pot luck, and hope for the best. They were wonderfully cunning on that battery, concealing·their guns in the most mysterious fashion. They must have had a position just outside a cave, and then, when they knew we were going to bombard, run their guns back, right inside the cavern, and so completely fogged us. They were always careful to fire when the sun was bearing near line, so as to make observation of the flash almost an impossibility. As for smoke, there didn't seem to be any. At Chenak they seemed to have mounted larger guns, for the "stuff" they sent over grew bigger every day.

Another day came and went, and still we came up for our daily christening. Only the old crocks remained now, and we didn't have a chance to give them the drubbing that we prayed for. For twenty-six days we had been under fire without a spell. Had any ship ever done better than this? The captain and the officers were beginning to feel the strain—there was no hiding the fact. Such a nerve-sapping torment as this leaves its mark despite the sturdiness of a man's heart.

The next morning (Friday, May 21st) we had hardly got anchored in the Straits when a regular inferno of fire greeted us. It was too risky to remain exposed on the upper deck, so all men immediately took cover. Bang!—a shell hit us squarely. It struck the starboard anchor bed, smashed one of the links of cable, and forced its way through the ship's side into the mess-deck, then through the lower mess-deck into the chain-locker, where it cut through three links of cable and —failed to explode.

Our gunnery officer went down into the chain locker and routed it out. It proved to be a 6 inch shell, and why it failed to explode we hadn't an opportunity of ascertaining, for it was taken solemnly to the side and dropped into the sea.

Again luck had favoured us. There were several narrow escapes, but no casualties. A man was washing himself on the upper messdeck when the visitor arrived. It passed down by the side of the tub of water in which he was washing, cut away a piece of the side and one hoop, and left the surprised washer unscathed. On the lower deck a man had his cap-box knocked out of his hand, and another man who was rolling dough on a table had it thrown all over him, the shell passing clean through the table, a foot or so from him.

It seemed that we were indeed a lucky ship. Had the shell burst on the mess-deck I dread to think of the consequences. Time after time we were hit after this, but thank God! no more shells came through the ship's side.

At 10 a.m. we received glorious news—we were going to be relieved at last! It seemed too good to be true, yet it proved to be the case, although our respite was to be of the briefest kind. We were to go to Mudros to coal and ammunition ship, and were to return on Sunday. Not much of a spell, but sufficient to fill every one with joy, and to set the ship buzzing with uncontrollable excitement. Who could wonder at it, when for twenty-seven continuous days and nights men's nerves had been strung to concert pitch, and every hour had been fraught with dangers of a dozen kinds? We remained for the rest of the forenoon bombarding the shore and at 12.30 left for Mudros, where we arrived safely at 6 p.m.

The place was crowded with ships of all descriptions, including eleven French men-of-war and several of our own. Altogether I counted over 280, so one can imagine what a sight it was. I noticed that there were no bumboats about, so concluded that either the natives had run short of food or they had made their fortunes and retired from business.

As soon as we were anchored the ammunition ship came alongside and we took in shell, etc., until 11 p.m. And then the crew, with glistening eyes, and inexpressible gratitude, went to a peaceful night's sleep.

CHAPTER XIII

THE LOSS OF THE "TRIUMPH"

WE were up at 4.30 next morning to coal ship—I think we could have slept for a century had we been allowed. No one seemed to realise what had happened; they walked about quite dazed with the sudden change. Men trod the forecastle with a strange, dubious look in their eyes, as though they doubted their senses. Where were the Turkish shells? Where was the daily strafing under which they had suffered for twenty-eight weary days? It certainly was difficult to realise that the danger had passed momentarily from us. And then, to cap the miracle, we heard that we were getting fresh meat and potatoes! For weeks we had lived on salt pork, and peas, bully beef and peas, provided and alternated with such persistency as to make our palates revolt at the very mention of it.

We were also lucky enough to buy some butter at 2s. 6d. per lb., and bacon at 2s. per lb., which were in the nature of a godsend, as we never hoped to see such luxuries again.

We finished coaling at 4 p.m. and didn't lose much time in seeking our hammocks, for sleep came as a wonderful balm, and we never knew how long it might be before we should sleep in comfort again. On the Sunday, to our intense delight, we were stopped from leaving, as submarines were lurking in the vicinity. We spent the day in giving the old ship a good scrub down, which she sorely needed. There was no time for church, but the Rev. Dawson held a Communion Service, this being his first opportunity since we last left Mudros.

I cannot help commenting upon this particular service, because one aspect of it struck one as being extraordinary. In that ship's company were men who had passed through the "valley of the shadow"—had seen Death gathering his grim harvest on every side. Men there were, who had given up every hope of life, and yet had escaped the danger that threatened them. All of them had been in that inferno for twenty-eight days, and had seen comrades swept to oblivion on an instant, and without the slightest warning, and yet, out of the whole ship's company, *the service was attended by exactly twenty!*

Who can solve this problem? The men were not ungrateful. I knew that. They had fought bravely and well, and would stick to their guns to the very last. Any one of them would have given his life to save a shipmate; and yet that Communion Service meant nothing to them. If those men did not feel that they owed thanksgiving to God for their lives, then it must be that the presence and reality of God has never been awakened within them. This point conceded, it follows that a tremendous work has yet to be done by the Church if it would make the teaching of Christ a reality, for these men could not be considered as negligible exceptions—they surely must be representative of a huge majority.

It is useless for me to seek an explanation. I can only leave it to those whose high calling it is to bring the message to man to find a cause and a remedy. There seems to be glorious work yet to be done, and I pray that the future may prove fruitful in this respect.

Our stay at Mudros was not much prolonged, owing to the presence of submarines; on Monday (May 24th) we received orders to proceed to the Dardanelles to take up our old position as bombarding ship. We were soon under way with eyes strained on the look-out for U-boats, for the poor old ship would prove easy prey for those sinister craft, it being difficult to get more than eleven knots out of her, which was practically as good as nothing at all.

Anyhow, we got there all right, and commenced our old tactics, the Turks greeting us with the usual "big stuff." At 8 p.m. we steamed outside and anchored for the night.

We heard that the "Vengeance" had a torpedo fired at her in the afternoon, when coming over from the base; so it seemed that the submarines meant business.

The next day a new job was allotted us. We were detailed to look after the left flank of the British and Indian troops operating to the north of Cape Hellas, as they were about to advance northwards along the coast. Pleased to get a change of work, we soon got the nets in, and proceeded to a position from which we could cover the advance party's operations.

THE LOSS OF THE "TRIUMPH" 165

It proved to be very tame, as we never so much as got a sight of a Turk. But at 12.22 p.m. a fresh catastrophe occurred. The "Triumph" was steaming about six miles ahead of us, off Gaba Tepe, when a torpedo struck her. We could see her very plainly from the bridge, broadside to us with her stern towards the land. Instantly she heeled over badly to the starboard. The destroyer "Chelmers" dashed up close to her port quarters, and the men from the "Triumph" began to march off her quarter-deck into the "Chelmers" forecastle. It was carried out in the most orderly fashion, and no one ignorant of the facts would have dreamed that it was anything other than a parade.

As far as we could see, the "Triumph" was holding steady, as though she was resting on the bottom—some of the crew jumped off her forecastle into the water, where a lot of trawlers and mine-sweepers were ready to pick them up.

Our belief that the "Triumph" was resting on the bottom proved to be false, for at 12.30, with a sudden rush, she turned completely over with her bottom in the air, and at 12.53 she disappeared from sight.

The T.B.D.'s and the few cruisers present

began steaming around like mad. Apparently they had sighted the submarine and were opening fire on her. Whether they hit her or not I do not know, but they were still on their quest when they disappeared from our range of vision. It appeared that the "Talbot" had also had a torpedo fired at her, but it missed and ran up on the beach, where it exploded.

The "Swiftsure" informed us that Rear-Admiral Stewart Nicholson was going to transfer his flag to us, and send the "Swiftsure" to the base, as she had no torpedo nets, and we had.

The Admiral transferred his flag to us, and we soon got under way, once more a flag-ship. The Admiral was a fine-looking man, and had brought all his staff aboard, so that really we had good cause to put on a few airs. We proceeded to Cape Hellas and anchored close in shore. What a change had taken place in the last few days! As far as I could see we were the only battleship left —all the others had cleared off to safer quarters, and so we lorded it in grand style, but we couldn't help thinking that our end must surely come, if we kept on, for there is an end even to the best of luck.

THE LOSS OF THE "TRIUMPH"

We heard that the "Triumph" had lost fifty-three men all told, which wasn't so bad considering all things. It became generally known that the Admiral was going to transfer his flag to the "Exmouth" as soon as she arrived, which news filled us with joy, for after that we were to proceed to Mudros without delay.

Towards night some fears were evidently felt for our safety, and we were instructed to proceed to Kapshalo for the night, as there was less danger there. We soon had our nets in and were off to Kapshalo.

We posted look-outs around the ship, set the gun-watches, and then piped down for the night.

At 1 a.m. I was awakened from the land of dreams by much noise and shouting, and, turning out, heard that a submarine had been seen inside the harbour defences. There was not much need to pipe "clear lower deck," for every man-jack was up and at his station for all emergencies. All of them had on our "dickey daws"—the name we had given to the Admiralty life-belts—all tied and ready for action. It turned out to be nothing more than a false alarm, the "submarine" proving to be one of our patrol boats returning to harbour.

We breathed again, and every one turned in, but I doubt if many of them got much sleep, for in their present "nervy" state, rumours and scares were not easily dismissed.

We remained in harbour until 11 a.m. and then proceeded to Seddul Bahr, where we anchored close in shore. We were practically surrounded by transports and minesweepers who were landing troops as fast as they could. We heard all kinds of rumours respecting the submarine; some said it had been sunk, but we hesitated to put much faith in the report, and were yearning for the "Exmouth" to arrive.

All the afternoon the Turks shelled Seddul Bahr village, from their elusive battery on the Asiatic side, but apparently not much damage was done.

In the evening we heard that the "Exmouth" was arriving the following day, and with a great sense of relief we anchored for the night, feeling that to-morrow we should be in Mudros.

CHAPTER XIV

THE LAST OF THE "MAJESTIC"

AT 5 o'clock the next morning (May 27th) I turned to, and, with the help of our six boys, gave the fore bridge a thorough clean down. This finished, we went to the after-bridge to clean that as well, but Commander Michael Barnes came up to get out the admiral's barge as the "Exmouth" was expected any moment. He was just giving the order for the port net to be got aft, when, coming round the bows of one of the troop-ships, and just off our port beam, we spotted a submarine. She was just astern of the mine-sweeper "Reindeer" with part of her conning tower and all her periscope above water. I immediately drew the commander's attention to it. He looked for a second and then said abruptly, "*Yes, and here comes the torpedo.*"

The commander shouted a warning to all

the men on the port side, and I shouted down the ventilator leading to the engine-room. The torpedo was travelling at a good rate, and I saw that it was going to strike somewhere forward, so I went to the end of the bridge to see the effect.

It struck! There was a great muffled roar and the old ship quivered and shook in a terrible way. The masts and yards swayed as if they were coming down on top of us, but they held good. A huge volume of water shot up for about 200 feet in the air, on the port side, and I knew that our end had come. Things began to move very quickly then. Men were running in every direction, but very quietly and swiftly, for they realised that we must fight for our lives, and that at any moment an internal explosion might ruin our last chance. The order was passed "every man for himself" and everything that would float was being commandeered as a possible aid to rescue. Every one seemed very cool, and there was scarcely any shouting. Overhead a French airman was hovering at about 200 feet, doubtless anxious to see what was happening. Tugs and trawlers were already coming to our assistance, but they couldn't come along-

THE LAST OF THE "MAJESTIC" 171

side as the ship had heeled over a lot to port, and it would have been dangerous for them. There was only one thing to do, and that was to swim for it. We had only one boat in the water, and that was tied up to the after-boom of the starboard net defence. She was soon full up with men—in fact, too full, but she got away all right. I took a hurried look around the after-bridge, but didn't see any one hurt at all, so I slipped down to the quarter-deck and went right aft. There was a wooden ladder secured to the hatchway which I cut away with my knife and threw overboard, thinking it might be the means of saving some one.

I possessed no life-belt, as I had left it below when I went up to clean the bridge. A French tug was approaching, and it seemed useless to remain on the ship longer, so I put the chin-stay of my cap under my chin, made sure that my trousers were securely fastened, took a last farewell of the dear old ship, and dived into a clear place, away from the crowd.

The water was gloriously warm, and, but for the dire circumstances, would have been a real treat. On looking round, I saw that one of the scuttles on the starboard quarter was open, so I swam back and looked into it. I shouted down but got no answer, and assumed that no one was down there. Just inside was an officer's cap which I secured and threw up to our chief buffer who was standing on the stern walk. A lot of other men were there, but they wouldn't dive in as they were under the impression that the ship was resting on the bottom. This I knew was not the case, for when I looked into the scuttles, the water inside was rising quickly—I told them this, and then swam for the French tug-boat which was now quite near—about thirty yards.

By the help of a rope I was soon on board her and ran forward to see what assistance I could be to the other men in the water. I found our commander and gunnery officer clearing away the small gun on the forecastle as the submarine was still visible in the distance, but before the gun could be got into action she had disappeared.

At that moment the "Majestic" made a final plunge and turned completely over, throwing all those that remained on deck into the water. The tug-boat went ahead a little in order to save as many lives as possible. I threw a heaving-line which was the means of saving six men—P.O. Stephens, P.O. (2nd Class Tar), Stoker Reese, and three others whose names I didn't hear, because no sooner had I pulled them in than I saw a man sinking near by. He was already under the surface, so there was no time to be lost. I dived in after him and was fortunate in getting him to the surface. The tug heaved me a line and eventually I got him aboard. He was in a very bad way, but we pumped him hard and used artificial respiration, which in the end brought him round. Poor chap! He had escaped death by a hair's-breadth, and looked ghastly. His name was McNeil, a R.N.R. man.

A good many of the others that we picked up had very narrow escapes. One man in particular—a stoker named Partridge—we worked on for a long time. He was practically gone when we picked him up and his head was hanging down in the water, only the lifebelt keeping him afloat. After a long time our work proved vain, as the doctor, when he arrived, assured us the poor chap was quite dead.

The captain was successful in saving two lives, although he had a narrow escape from losing his own.

The dear old ship had proved game to the last and finished her career with the admiral's flag still flying. In four and a half minutes she settled down, but with a portion of her keel still showing forward. Even when we left her—for good—this last portion of her still protruded from the water. One man who was on board when she lurched over was thrown up on the unsubmerged keel, and it looked almost comic to see him sitting there in solitary state, thanking God, I doubt not, for his good fortune.

Some of the crew had landed on the beach and others were on tugs, mine-sweepers, T.B.D.'s, and the various other craft that had participated in the work of rescue. It was impossible, then, to gauge the loss of lives, but from what I saw we didn't seem to have fared so badly.

The tug's party, with a lot of others, were transferred to the fleet-sweeper "Reindeer," for passage to Mudros. We took our dead with us and buried them at sea on the journey as the Rev. Dawson was with us. I shall never forget that service. I think the padre felt it more than any of us, and it was obvious to us that he had to summon every ounce of his courage to save breaking down.

What with the loss of the ship, and the sight of our comrades being consigned to their last resting-place, it was a bitter potion for those of us that were left, and one calculated to tear the heartstrings of the strongest.

On board the ship there were many stories of wonderful escapes, and to relate a tithe of them would more than double my narrative. One man—Stoker Sullivan, P.O.—was in the stokehold when the torpedo struck. He was standing under a grating, and the explosion threw him into the air. He grabbed wildly at anything, and by good fortune his fingers hooked into the grating—which would be about twenty feet up. He went along this hand over hand, and reached the nearest ladder, which brought him to the upper deck just in time to feel the ship go over to port with a rush. There was a great swirl of water, and then he remembered no more until he came to on board one of the tugs. His skin was flaming red all over as though it had been cooked, but he swore he felt all right. So far as we knew he was the only man to escape from the port stokehold.

Other men, when the ship rolled over, had been jammed between the starboard nets and the ship's side, and were caught like rats in a trap, but when the ship took her final roll over the nets fell clear of her, and as most of the men had their rubber life-belts blown up, they came to the surface again. A lot of the men who couldn't swim had hung on to the last moment, not believing that the ship would roll over.

We must have looked a queer lot on board the "Reindeer," for some were wrapped up in blankets, and others clad in all kinds of garb—half soldiers, half sailors—while a few were still in their flannels and drawers, just as they had come out of the water. But the paymaster was busy hunting up every scrap of clothing he could find, and those who were not lucky enough to get a full suit had no cause for complaint, for it was a gloriously warm day with the sun shining from a spotless sky.

We were a large company, for, besides 210 of the "Majestic" crew, there were a lot of wounded soldiers going back to the base, and some very bad cases among them, which caused us to think less of our own sorrows.

We arrived at Mudros at 3 p.m. and were transferred to s.s. "Saturna," one of the Donaldson line boats. Here we found a lot

THE LAST OF THE "MAJESTIC" 177

more of our men who had been brought over by French and British T.B.D.'s, also the crew of the poor old "Triumph."

There was nothing to do but settle down and wait events. So we got hammocks served out to us, and sat down to an excellent tea of real fresh butter and jam and bread, such as we had not tasted for many a long day.

Everybody was sending home cables to inform relatives that they had been saved, but I doubt if any of them reached their destination—mine didn't.

I heard that forty-five of the crew had been lost in all. All of our signalling staff were saved except one, a wireless boy called "Peg." He was a good swimmer, but appeared to have lost his life in a struggle with a drowning man whom he tried to save.

We were all proud of the old "Majestic," for she had finished her career after covering herself with glory. She was the first battleship to enter the Dardanelles, and she was the last to remain there. We were the battleship to escort the first Canadian contingent to England, and we had tasted battle in its most violent form. Singularly enough our captain, Fitzroy Talbot, had served in her as a midshipman in his early days.

The "Majestic" was the sixth ship I had seen go down. "Bouvet," "Irresistible," "Ocean," "Goliath," "Triumph," and our own dear ship, and I earnestly hope I shall witness no more such catastrophes. These sights live for ever in the memory, and are a ghastly nightmare. One cannot shake off the horror of it all—the struggling masses of humanity, half naked, clinging to anything that would offer support—the despairing cries, and the visions of homes in quiet country villages all unconscious of the fate that had overwhelmed their dear ones. One can only give the thing in its broadest outline; there are the thousand and one details, each pitiful in itself, that cannot be told in full. There were men in the stokeholds that never had a dog's chance, but were drowned like rats, though their hearts were the stoutest that men ever possessed. In one case there were two men who had lived through all the terrors of the shipwreck, and had swam and struggled to land, only to reach it and drop down dead from their exertions.

No wonder the men around me were silent and haggard of face! It was not only the loss of their ship and their comrades, it was the cumulative effect of days and nights under fire, without a moment's respite—a mental strain such as surely no body of men have endured since the world began. When the climax came, it shattered the last thread of fortitude within them, and left them paralysed with the magnitude of their misfortune.

I should have mentioned earlier that when I dived off the ship the last thing that caught my eye was the figure of Mr. Ashmead Bartlett standing on the bridge, coolly looking at his watch to time the occurrence of the disaster !

CHAPTER XV

HOME AGAIN

THE next morning (May 28th) we awoke feeling greatly refreshed after a good night's sleep. We were all served out with soldiers' khaki clothing, and the result was rather funny, as they were evidently made for small men, and not at all adapted to sailors with big waist lines. However, we were not very fastidious about our clothes just then, and were quite satisfied in having anything at all to wear.

For a few days we did very little but recuperate after our terrible experiences. A lot of bad cases of nervous breakdown were sent off to Malta in a hospital ship, and the rest of us were left to speculate upon our next destination.

On June 1st a tug came alongside and we were taken aboard her, but we didn't remain on her long, for at 10 a.m. we were signalled for by the "Saturna," and learnt that we were to leave for England in the "Carmenia" of Cap Trafalgar fame, which was lying at Mudros.

It might be imagined that such news as this would be received with exultation by the men, but strangely enough it created just the opposite impression. They wanted badly enough to see their wives and families again, but they wanted, before that, to see their present job through. They were hungry for revenge upon the Turk for the miseries that they had suffered, and they wanted to see the Union Jack flying right through the Narrows into the Sea of Marmora and up to Constantinople itself.

But I think that, underneath all their zest, was a feeling that the thing couldn't be done, and that preparation and geographical advantages had given the Turk overwhelming strength.

At 5 p.m. we left the "Saturna," and got on board the "Carmenia," which was due to sail that night. I was afraid some of our fellows would get left behind, but, as luck would have it, the "Carmenia" did not sail that night after all, and in the morning a few more stragglers arrived. The following morning we left Mudros for Malta, carrying fully two thousand men on board which detracted from our comfort very considerably ; but we made the best of it, being glad in our hearts that we were *en route* for dear old England.

A band of a French man-of-war played us out of the harbour and some destroyers accompanied us for a short distance out to sea, and then we proceeded on our own, maintaining a zigzag course all the time. A good many look-outs were posted round the ship and these were supplemented by an army of volunteers who didn't like the idea of being taken unawares by a submarine. All the signal-staff of the "Triumph" and "Majestic" were employed on the bridge, but there weren't many of them, for a lot had not been able to get back from the various places to join the ship before she sailed. We had a few exercises at boat-drill in case of accident, and all had cork life-belts served out to meet any emergency.

The question of feeding us all was a serious one, for the ship had not been prepared to carry such a large crowd of men. Meals had to be taken in four reliefs and a fine old crush it was too. Some of our men still suffered

HOME AGAIN

from shock, and would not go below for their meals as it was a long way down, and they were afraid of another accident. Nothing would move them, so the only alternative was to bring their meals up to them, which was rather a monotonous job, several times a day.

For three days we steamed across a calm blue sea without any untoward incident occurring, and on the morning of June 4th Malta hove in sight. The signalling station at Castella challenged us, and, on receiving our reply, informed us what buoy we were to go to. We steamed up the grand harbour and were soon at anchor, thankful that one span of sea was safely overcome and joyfully conscious that the white cliffs of England were appreciably nearer.

No sooner did we arrive than a collier steamed alongside and Maltese began to coal ship. All day this went on, and, as they had not finished when daylight vanished, we stayed in harbour for the night. There had been rumours going around that we were not going to England after all, and it was with great relief that late in the evening the men learned that the "Carmenia" really was taking us to England.

Malta was much changed from when I had seen it last. Then it was a hive of industry, French and British ships thronged the grand harbour, and altogether the place presented the appearance of great importance. But now the harbour was empty save for a few ships undergoing repairs, and the whole aspect was completely changed. Somehow it had an air of sadness, and the hospital cases that were constantly being discharged there served to enhance its melancholia.

We finished coaling at 3.30 the next day, and half an hour later were steaming out of the grand harbour, homeward bound.

All was very quiet in the Mediterranean. On the 8th we passed Gibraltar on our zig-zag course, praying that submarines would give us a wide berth.

The voyage continued favourably and all went well with us, save for a mysterious malady which attacked almost every member of the ship. It took the form of violent stomachic troubles, and men writhed in agony. Nobody discovered the cause of it, but we had shrewd ideas that the doctors knew a lot about it, and had "prepared" our food for some reason or other. When the men went to them they only screwed up their mouths and assured them it would be better soon—and so it was, but it frightened the life out of the poor chaps while it lasted.

We passed Ushant one evening at 6 p.m., but we were too far out to see the land.

We passed a few steam trawlers on patrol duty, who signalled to us; but we had nothing to report, and passed on our way, almost unable to control the ever-growing excitement within us.

Soon the news got round that we were making for Plymouth, and a fine murmur of joy went up. Plymouth! even the sound of the word made our hearts beat faster within us. We could hardly realise that only a few days ago we were struggling for our lives in enemy waters, and now, the uttermost hope of our hearts was near to being realised.

Every one was asking the same questions. "How fast were we steaming?" "When should we arrive?" "Should we meet an escort?" They had let the thought of home grow in their minds, and it became obsessing.

June 12th will never be forgotten by the men that came back in the "Carmenia." I lay in my hammock for two hours, unable to gain a wink of sleep for the excitement which possessed me. When midnight came and the glorious 12th was ushered in I went on deck, and there found the men standing about in groups, strangely silent. No one wanted to talk, and when a man moved he walked with a light step, as though fearing to disturb the thoughts of his comrades.

The ship was making fine progress up Channel, and in the darkness we waited, almost counting the revolutions of the propellers. The half-hour struck—what a terribly long half-hour! It seemed an eternity; Time seemed to be lagging in the most torturesome way. Another half-hour, and another, and then, after a period of what seemed centuries, the look-out man reported land on the starboard bow.

All hands were up in an instant, wondering what land it could be, especially on the starboard bow, as we should have seen land ahead on the port bow first going up Channel.

But the ship had made even better progress than we had calculated, and as we had been given the time for entering the Sound, the captain had run the ship up the coast a bit, as far as the Start Light, which accounted for the land being sighted on the starboard bow, as we were running down Channel again.

It was dear old Devon that had been sighted, the land that many of us had known from childhood. We made good progress, and soon left Prawle Point behind us. Bolt Head and Bolt Trail were passed, and the sentinel of the Sound, the Eddystone, loomed up in the distance. At Stokes Point they challenged us, and we passed on our way.

Plymouth Sound opened out wide in the distance, and my heart gave a great bound. It seemed that it couldn't be true, and was only a dream, the dream that I had dreamt a hundred times before. But, as the distance lessened, and the familiar land-marks loomed up, it became a dream no longer, but a glorious reality. The sun was just climbing over the horizon and everything was exquisitely peaceful.

Home! It was the first time that I had realised the word in its fulness. Only those who have almost given up hope of seeing home again can know what it means to see the dear familiar cliffs beckoning, welcoming, in the hush of a summer morning, with the green trees nodding on the hills and the corn waving in the valleys.

I remembered that it was my wife's birthday, and was glad to know that the birthday present she would get was the one she would desire above all things—even if it was only me.

We entered the western entrance to the Sound and proceeded up to the Hamoaze. The Devon men were pointing out the old familiar things that it was so good to see again, and were almost like children in their immeasurable delight.

We were all mad to get ashore. At 7 a.m. breakfast was ready, but very few men touched any—such mundane things were far from their thoughts just then.

At 7.45 we fell in on the jetty with all our belongings slung across our backs, and from there marched to the Royal Naval Barracks which was only a few minutes away. We all assembled in the drill-shed, where we had to wait until we got told off for our messes; but, as I knew the run of the R.N.B., I slipped away and sent a wire to my wife wishing her many happy returns of the day, and telling her I was coming home. My only regret was that I was not present to see her face when that telegram arrived and was read.

The officer at the post office looked at me

HOME AGAIN

very hard when he read the telegram, and then could hardly speak for the tears in his eyes as he recognised me as a boy in the old "Lion" when he was instructor there. He absolutely insisted upon paying for the telegram, and was much affected by the memories which my identity revived in his mind.

The next few hours were all rush. We got our gear put away, saw the doctor, and then rushed for the train.

There is little more to tell. What followed is entirely personal, and I and the other men were repaid a thousandfold for the toil and strain of those weary months. Some of us will doubtless fight again before the enemy is crushed, and for that day we wait patiently and hopefully, trusting in God and our Cause.

FINIS

www.ingramcontent.com/pod-product-compliance
Lightning Source LLC
Chambersburg PA
CBHW071003160426
43193CB00012B/1897